Happy Baking!

Carol G. Drud

# i knew you were coming
# were coming

*so i baked a*

# cake

More Than 140 Recipes for Delectable Desserts
That Make a Big Impression with a Minimum of Effort

# CAROL G. DURST

SIMON & SCHUSTER

Simon & Schuster
Rockefeller Center
1230 Avenue of the Americas
New York, NY 10020

SIMON & SCHUSTER and colophon are registered trademarks
of Simon & Schuster Inc.

Designed by Bonni Leon-Berman

Manufactured in the United States of America

1  3  5  7  9  10  8  6  4  2

Library of Congress Cataloging-in-Publication Data

Durst, Carol G.
I knew you were coming, so I baked a cake : more than 140 recipes
for delectable desserts that make a big impression with a minimum of
effort / Carol G. Durst.
p.    cm.
Includes index.
1. Desserts.    I. Title.
TX773.D825    1997
641.8'6—dc21    97-23889
CIP

ISBN 0-684-81490-0

This book is dedicated to my family, all of whom ate their share, shared their care, and cheered me on.

And, especially, this book is for my son, William, who brought me a copy of my favorite children's book, *The Duchess Bakes a Cake,* by Virginia Kahl, asking me to bake "a lovely, light luscious, delectable cake." I tried, Will.

# acknowledgments

First, I wish to thank my friend Pat Baird, who got me to feed 3,000 runners one week, and who continues to get me into more mischief than I ever believe is possible.

Then, my agent, Alice Martell, who believed in me from the very first snowstorm, shared her ideas, and coached me to completion. What a champion! What support!

To Sydny Miner, my editor, who sensed when to push and was always kind enough to "lay off."

For the support I received from Leslie Revsin, Helene Bass-Wichelhaus, and "The Group."

To Nick Malgieri, my first baking teacher, who always delivers even more than he promises, and who exemplifies the intelligence, skill, and finesse I most admire in culinary professionals.

Thanks to those who shared recipes: Helene Bass-Wichelhaus, Amy Cotler, Anita Farber, the Gurfields, Nick Malgieri, Alice Martell, Sabrina Shear, the Wolfes, my neighbor Gretta (although her family's almond cake is not here, the flavor is), and my folks.

Thanks to those who read the unedited manuscript, for their generosity of time and comments: Pat Baird, Flo Braker, Amy Cotler, Nick Malgieri, Sara Moulton, Leslie Revsin, Andy Schloss, Michele Urvater, and, of course, Mom.

Thanks also to those who tasted the unedited products, all those friends and neighbors who got me through the hundreds of "little moments," especially the Blooms, Knight-Greenfields, Doskows, and Guajuardos.

Thanks to Anna Sewhoy for typing, typing, tasting, and typing.

And thanks to Les, for helping me find the determination to complete this work.

It's quite a project, a "little book."

# contents

contents

**9**

# introduction

**I'm a working mom,** living a too-hectic, demanding life, and I still want to entertain friends and family. I want to make the biggest, most delicious impression for the least investment in time, effort, and sometimes cost—the psychic cost, mostly, of us overworked, overscheduled, overplanned, yet nurturing souls.

*I Knew You Were Coming So I Baked a Cake* is about my belief that homemade is still important. The recipe ideas and strategies in this book will help you step into your kitchen and create something that tastes good, that doesn't look or feel as though it came off an assembly line, and that expresses your caring and effort. It is about the fun of making something delicious—quickly and easily.

This book is about *easy, easy, easy!* It uses easy-to-find ingredients, and all the needed equipment is readily available at any market. It has easy-to-put-together recipes in small steps that you can do ahead, ten minutes at a time. The recipes are not messy or complex. Even cleanup is easy.

These recipes will enable you to make a wide range of desserts in the time it would take to stop at a bakery and buy one. Some of these desserts have real old-fashioned charm; most feature new-fangled techniques and simplicity, using special products or shortcuts to make them *fast.*

I recommend certain flavor combinations and describe basic preparations that set you up with techniques to make many recipes. These Building Block recipes are coded with this special symbol . In running text, the Building Block recipes have been printed in **bold type.**

There are cross-references and suggestions throughout the book so you can find all the elements you liked to combine. Substitutions appear in many recipes, in case you find yourself in the middle of a recipe but lack a particular ingredient. There are doughs that can be frozen to give you a jump on filling, slicing, and baking "fresh" cookies or tarts, and parts of recipes are clearly marked *"do ahead."*

You'll find ideas to meet many special needs cross-referenced in the Special-Needs List on pages 205–13.

You can fit baking into your crazy, busy schedule. Not Aunt Tillie's rugelach on a weeknight, but with a well-stocked pantry, some Building Block recipes, and a

introduction

few steps planned ahead, something homemade, loving, and wonderful can come out of your kitchen oven anytime.

## taste memory

I am very lucky to come from a family with a great heritage in baking and cooking, not to mention eating. I have a mom who always saved a bit of pie crust for me so I could roll out a little one of my own. I have a dad who always claimed to taste our feet in the cookies we made, and patiently ate his way through anything and everything we three sisters produced as we earned our Girl Scout badges.

My father's mom, all five feet of her, baked and cooked for boarders who came to their farm in the Catskill Mountains during the summer to escape New York City heat. Without refrigeration or commercial cooking equipment, and certainly not using a cookbook (she owned none and couldn't read English), she was still renowned as a fine baker.

Perhaps the fact that she baked each and every day earned her that fame. Perhaps she knew her equipment, knew what she could do, and cleverly rotated her repertoire. She made items that didn't mind a little hot spot in the oven, things that could be "fixed" with a dollop of fresh whipped cream, or items in which the definition of "good" did not depend on appearance. "Good" for Grandma meant, "It tastes good; your stomach doesn't care what it looks like."

I share this lore with you, in deference to our baking mothers, fathers, and teachers, holding tight to the values of homemade.

## what's a good dessert?

A good dessert meets several criteria, including:

**TASTE**   Sweet, tart, fruity, or chocolaty; does it make you say "Mmm"?

**TEXTURE**   A tender crumb, a crisp pastry, the feel on the tongue, how something fills the mouth and changes with temperature as it melts, all contribute to our enjoyment.

**CONTRAST**   The skilled handling of different ingredients, the successful combinations of flavor, color, and texture.

**EYE APPEAL**   How it pleases the eye, enhanced by placement on the plate, decoration, and garnishes.

i knew you were coming so i baked a cake

All the desserts in this book meet these standards. In addition, I added several practical considerations to my working definition of "good":

· Does the recipe (almost) always work?
· Does the recipe work for friends who say they aren't regular bakers?
· Are all the ingredients readily available?
· Can this be made in different shapes, quantities, and sizes to accommodate equipment most people have in their homes (or can get at their local housewares store)?
· Will (almost) everyone like it?
· Can this be used in several ways?
· Can this be made (or started) ahead of time, in ten-minute segments?
· Is the mess minimal?
· Can I keep extras (or parts) in the freezer?
· Does this smell good? Does this product release a fragrance that says "homemade"?

## practice

As I began this book, my stomach was in knots. I know how to feed 800 people in the middle of a park, but I wasn't so sure about writing a book. I took it one recipe at a time, and I kept on changing, collecting, trying, retrying. As with Mr. Goodyear's scales for the piano, practicing did develop technique. With each success I developed new skills, self-confidence, and speed. The second or third time I tackled a recipe I knew what I was comparing. I knew why I was choosing one less step and how to describe the procedure more clearly.

So I thought I would share this basic truth with you: If you do bake more, you *will* bake more, because it gets easier with practice and faster with familiarity, and it's enormously satisfying.

Have fun. I wish you many happy minutes of baking and many contented guests in your home.

introduction

# getting started

The art and skill of professional bakers is built on a series of basic preparations, which can then be embellished or combined to create many different products.

I have used that concept in this book. If you can master several simple basic preparations, and I know you can, then the combinations and creations are as endless as your imagination. All the basic preparations are starred with this symbol 🌸 so you can watch for the Building Blocks that you'll use again and again.

Many recipes have steps you can *Do Ahead* or *Quick Tips* to speed you along, and each one identifies equipment you will need to prepare the recipe. Many recipes have parts you can keep on hand, or are made up of parts you can assemble at the last minute. There's a whole chapter for products you can find readily at the grocery store and then enhance with your personal touch.

## stocking up

| building-block recipes (🌸 symbol) | |
| --- | --- |
| almond torte | fruit purées |
| biscuits | lemon curd |
| butter cake | meringues |
| buttercream | nick malgieri's no-roll pie crust |
| cream cheese cookie dough | oatmeal pecan crisp topping |
| cream cheese icing | pâte sucre |
| cream puffs | nut brittle or praline |
| crêpes | vanilla pudding |
| "don't do it" chocolate cake | whipped cream |
| dulce de leche | |

## ingredients

Assembling ingredients and equipment can take most of your time, but not if you organize a baking shelf. If everything is within reach, making it so easy, you will bake much more readily.

i knew you were coming so i baked a **cake**

14

Only good ingredients make the finished product worth the effort. Trying to use up some old flour in the cupboard resulted in several rotten cakes as I started testing recipes for this book. Remaking the same recipe with fresh(er) ingredients (who knows how long packages sit on the grocer's shelf?) made a big difference in the results. So throw away old stuff, or you'll waste your efforts and get discouraged. Buy the best quality products to start with, and use only *genuine* (not artificial) chocolate, extracts, spices, and liqueurs.

Tastes, textures, and smells seduce you into baking. Your memories, or the wish to create those "home-baked" memories for someone else, make the effort worthwhile.

*Talk to your cookbook.* Make notes along its borders so you can personalize a recipe, and note changes in procedure or substitutions for ingredients. It really saves me time if I am reminded that I used yogurt in a recipe calling for buttermilk, or how much extra cinnamon I added.

Flour, egg whites, puff pastry, and even chocolate all behave differently in humid weather conditions. On some days a recipe may need a little extra flour or longer beating. Things also change at high altitudes. So, while measuring accurately and following each step are important the first time you approach a cake recipe, experience and making notes in your book will help you adapt your techniques to your environment.

Following are the ingredients I suggest you keep on hand. Several recipes require special ingredients, perhaps a fruit liqueur or candy bar, which will have to be purchased to make that one dessert. However, the ingredients are readily available at grocery stores, and most can be stored on your shelves or in your refrigerator or freezer for months.

## pantry—keep it on the shelf

### chocolates:

unsweetened chocolate—This holds indefinitely on the shelf and is essential for brownies. The one ounce premelted "Chocolate Flavor" "Choco Bake" is not *real* chocolate. If the convenience of saving one step helps you make brownies, the microwave recipe will work with the premelted packets.

semisweet chocolate—Nothing fixes my chocolate cravings like fine semisweet chocolate. Combined with butter and cream in varying proportions, it can become a chocolate glaze or a cake icing, a fudge sauce, a truffle mix, or a rich tart filling.

cocoa powder—You cannot substitute hot chocolate mix for cocoa powder, which is pure chocolate liquor with the moisture removed. Hot chocolate mix adds sugar and sometimes milk solids, which confuses the proportions.

milk chocolate—Often preferred as a cookie or confection ingredient, it's not usually used in cake batter.

white chocolate—Not really chocolate, but it adds variety to cookies, blondies, or confections. It is available in chips for easy use and quick melting.

Nutella—This chocolate-hazelnut spread is a European standby. It makes a sophisticated cake filling and can be used to enhance a puff pastry dessert or finish a cupcake with a soft swirl, ready for sprinkles. It also makes a terrific snack if simply spread on bread.

### flours:
all-purpose flour—All-purpose flour is used throughout this book unless otherwise specified. If sifting makes you cranky, measure 1 level cup of flour and remove 1 rounded tablespoon—you are close enough!

cake flour—I don't use self-rising cake flour. It contains baking powder in amounts determined by the manufacturer, and this can really mess up your recipe. If you can find a cake flour without baking powder added, be sure to tell your supplier you want it kept in stock.

cornstarch—This is used to thicken puddings, to add body to fruit purées, or to lighten flour for cake flour. You may substitute ¾ cup all-purpose flour and 2 tablespoons cornstarch for 1 cup of cake flour.

### leavening:
baking powder—Use this in most cakes and muffins.

baking soda—This leavener is used with acidic ingredients such as molasses, buttermilk, orange juice, honey.

### sugars:
confectioners' sugar—10X, the finest powdered sugar, dissolves most rapidly in liquid. Dusted over the top of a cake, it's an easy, attractive, instant decoration.

i knew you were coming so i baked a cake

white sugar—Granulated sugar is used throughout this book unless something else is specified.

light brown sugar—This is granulated sugar cut by the manufacturer with a bit of molasses. I prefer light brown sugar for Blondies, for crisp toppings, and in peach desserts.

dark brown sugar—Granulated sugar cut with more molasses than light brown sugar, this has the richest taste, and it is my preference for Granny's Oatmeal Cookies, a burnt sugar "brûlée" topping, or Butterscotch Sauce.

molasses—A by-product of the sugar refining process, it adds that dark, rich undertone to Gingerbread and Granny's Oatmeal Cookies.

light corn syrup—This is used mostly for confections such as Nut Brittle.

maple syrup—I think everything from breakfast waffles to Crêpes to Blondies is best with 100 percent natural U.S. Grade A Dark Amber maple syrup. Nothing less really does it for me.

This list includes the goods required for *every* dessert in this book. Obviously, you don't need every item listed here; pick the ingredients and flavors you like best, to start. I've starred the ones I like to keep on hand.

**canned fruits**
Apple, blueberry, and/or cherry pie filling
Apricots
Blackberries
Blueberries
*Cherries
Kadota figs
*Pears
Peaches

**dry fruits**
*Apricots
Blueberries
Cherries

*Cranberries
*Currants
*Dates
Figs
*Golden raisins
*Peaches
Pears
Prunes (pitted)
*Raisins

## *graham crackers or crumbs

Three packs in a 1-pound box will yield enough crumbs for three cheesecakes or three pies. The packaged crumbs yield enough for three cheesecakes as well, although the boxes weigh a bit less.

## extracts
*Almond
*Vanilla

## jams
*Apricot
Cherry
Prune (*lekvar*)
*Raspberry

## wines and spirits

There are many domestic wines, sherries, and flavored brandies that will work just fine in baking. But if you happen to have a fine liqueur in the house, it will certainly enhance your dessert. Imported products are generally more expensive. Below are the items used in this book, which your local liquor store will certainly be able to offer in your price range.

Banana
Bourbon
*Brandy
Cherry
*Coffee

i knew you
were coming
so i baked a
cake

*Currant
Fortified Wines: Madeira, Port, or Sherry
Melon
*Orange
Peach
Pear
*Raspberry
*Rum
Scotch whiskey
Sparkling wines

## spices
Allspice
Cardamom
*Cinnamon
*Crystallized ginger
Dried lemon and orange peel
*Ground cloves
*Ground ginger
*Ground nutmeg

## miscellaneous
*All kinds of chips—various chocolates, butterscotch, peanut butter, etc.
Almond paste
Candied fruits
*Chocolate syrup
*Condensed milk—whole, low-fat, or nonfat
*Cooking spray
Cranberry sauce
Earl Grey tea
*Espresso powder
*Food coloring
*Gelatin
Glacéed fruits
*Honey
*Mandarin orange segments
Maraschino cherries

*Oatmeal
*Peanut butter
Rosewater
*Variety of sprinkles
*White vinegar

## keep it in the refrigerator

I use full-fat dairy products unless it is specified in the recipe that low-fat or non-fat can be substituted. In general, recipes require some fat to carry flavors and to incorporate or bind ingredients together, and this is dessert, so live a little.

**BUTTER**    Sweet, unsalted AA quality is used throughout these recipes.

**BUTTERMILK**    Cultured low-fat buttermilk has about 1.5% milk fat, active cultures, and no salt added, which makes this a tangy way to keep fats low in Anita Farber's Banana Cake.

**COTTAGE CHEESE**    Used in this book for Coeur à la Crème and a crêpe filling, any fat content (or nonfat) will work. If cottage cheese is used in other baking, some fat content helps carry flavors.

**CREAM CHEESE**    In cheese cake, tiramisù, and icings, I use the full-fat version—the fats add body and texture to these desserts. Spread reduced-fat cream cheese on your breakfast toast.

**CRÈME FRAÎCHE**    A thick, cultured cream. Both imported and domestic products are available in specialty-food shops. It can easily be made at home with a half cup heavy cream stirred into a half cup sour cream. Cover and leave at room temperature 10 to 12 hours. Stir, and refrigerate for another day before using.

**EGGS**    All the recipes in this book use large eggs—which yield one ounce of egg white and one ounce of yolk by American standard measures. Eggs yield differently according to their sizes, so if you've purchased medium, extra-large, or jumbo eggs, you'll need to convert by volume to execute the recipes properly. Break the egg into a clear Pyrex measuring cup (if the recipe calls for whole egg), beat the egg gently, and spoon off the amount in excess of the two-ounce standard for large eggs. You'll need to use three medium eggs in a recipe calling for two large eggs, and remove a bit from two extra-large or jumbo eggs to measure the equivalent of two large eggs.

**HEAVY CREAM**    Preferably pasteurized, not ultrapasteurized.

**MARGARINE OR SOLID SHORTENING**    I prefer one based on corn oil.

i knew you
were coming
so i baked a
cake

**MASCARPONE**   A sweet, dense, fresh Italian cheese, similar to cream cheese but richer and lighter in texture. Use cream cheese with heavy cream as a substitute in tiramisù.

**MILK**   I generally use whole milk in baking, but cakes and puddings in this book can all be made with low-fat milk, and in specified recipes with nonfat (skim) milk.

**RICOTTA CHEESE**   Although ricotta is available in supermarkets, I prefer the handmade fresh product found in specialty stores or traditional Italian neighborhood markets.

**SOUR CREAM**   Grade A pasteurized carries almost 20 percent butterfat, so sweetened or unsweetened, this is rich in or on any dessert.

**YOGURT**   Low-fat or reduced-fat is fine in any recipe in this book. Strawberry-Yogurt Muffins and Anita Farber's Banana Cake can be made with nonfat yogurt, because there are enough other fats in the recipe.

**time-savers to keep in the refrigerator**
Dried Fruit Compotes (page 172)
Dulce de Leche (page 75)
Lemons and lemon zest

## keep it in the freezer

Bananas
Blueberries, cranberries, raspberries
Butter, sweet, unsalted AA quality
Fruits: cherries, peaches, rhubarb
Lemon juice and zest
Nuts: almonds, cashews, coconut, hazelnuts, peanuts, pecans, pistachios, walnuts
Orange juice concentrate
Phyllo pastry
Puff pastry

**building block recipes that hold in the freezer**
Almond Torte
Anita Farber's Banana Cake
Biscuits (baked)
Butter Cake Layers
Buttercream, flavored or unflavored

Coeur à la Crème
Cream Cheese Pastry (unbaked)
Cream Puffs (baked)
Fruit Purées
Oatmeal Pecan Crisp Topping (unbaked)
Pâte Sucre Pastry (unbaked)

## pantry time savers

I recycle jars from mustards, jams, and mayonnaise to hold combinations of ingredients I use often. Preparing these mixtures will save you time when you need to finish fast. I think you will be more inclined to start a baking project if you know part is already assembled and right on your pantry shelf.

### cinnamon-sugar

I always keep a mixture of ½ cup of sugar and 1 to 1½ teaspoons cinnamon in a wide-mouthed jar, because I reach for this almost as often as I reach for granulated sugar. Cinnamon-Sugar tops Baked Apples, Cookies, Sour Cream Coffee Cake, Apple Kuchen, fruit tarts and pies, crisps, crêpes, and graham cracker crusts. You'll think of more ways to use it, if it's there.

### mixed spices

For the fastest Spiced Nuts, a flavorful Peach Crisp, or Apple Purée, measure these ingredients directly into a jar, put on the lid, and give it a shake.

> ½ cup sugar
> ¼ teaspoon salt
> 1 teaspoon cinnamon
> ½ teaspoon allspice
> ½ teaspoon ground ginger
> ½ teaspoon ground nutmeg
> ½ teaspoon ground cloves

### cake or muffin mix

I like to make my own mixes, omitting the BHT, extra salt, and mystery ingredients often found in commercial packages. Measure flour, baking powder or baking soda, and salt for your favorite cakes or muffins into jars or zip-top bags. *Label it* so you know which recipe, which cookbook, and which page you need to find again. Put the jar on a cool, dark shelf, or in the back of the refrigerator. This saves the time of cleaning up the flour dust I usually create with measuring and pouring. These mixes will easily hold for two months or longer if the flour was not stored a long time at the grocer's.

### chocolate fudge pudding mix

This mix can be used to make the Chocolate Fudge Pudding on page 149 and gives you a jump start on Tiramisù, page 157. The proportions given here are for a single serving; simply multiply them to fill your airtight container. To make one serving, add 5 tablespoons of this mix to 1 cup of milk and proceed with the recipe.

> 2 tablespoons cocoa
> 2 tablespoons sugar
> I tablespoon cornstarch

### cake flour

To make 1 cup of cake flour, measure, mix together, label, and store in a jar or zip-top bag:

> ¾ cup flour
> 2 tablespoons cornstarch

## the arguments for and against cake mixes

First, there's nothing wrong with them. They are fine. I feel they are on a par with white bread: They serve their purpose and all's well that gets eaten.

I baked mixes alongside homemade cakes, and most of my unsuspecting tasters found them fine, though they preferred the homemade product. They took more note of the icings or accompaniments than the cakes themselves, just as with a sandwich made on white bread, you notice the sandwich *filling*, not what encloses it.

But why not make cakes from scratch?

"Well, they take more time." Not these cakes.

"But there are so many steps." Not these recipes.

"But there's so much measuring." By the time I had broken eggs, measured milk or water and oil, had beaten, stirred, and poured the mixes into the pans, *the difference came down to measuring flour, baking soda or baking powder, and salt.* So premeasure amounts needed for several homemade cakes and scoop them into jars or zip-top bags, *labeled,* for the day when you want to bake but don't want to clean up the flour mess.

"Flour makes such a mess." This is true. So if you *must* sift, sift onto wax paper and make clean-up easy, or try some of the desserts in this book that don't require any flour. There are lots to choose from.

---

## equivalents and substitutions

Throughout this book, specific alternative ingredients and flavorings are suggested. There are a few generic swaps to mention:

Sour Cream, buttermilk, or yogurt work much the same and can be exchanged in equal volume in Sour Cream Coffee Cake and Anita Farber's Banana Cake, but the butterfat and body that sour cream, crème fraîche, cream cheese, or mascarpone offers are best for toppings and garnishes.

If you lack yogurt, sour cream, or buttermilk, you can sour one cup of whole milk with a 1/2 tablespoon of lemon juice or white vinegar.

The puddings and cake batters that use cornstarch do not need the butterfat of whole milk, so low-fat or even skim milk will work well. The Chocolate Fudge Pudding is even better using chocolate milk.

Icings can be made with heavy cream, sour cream, or cream cheese, so use what you have, with sufficient fat content to adhere firmly to the cake.

Condensed milk recipes work with nonfat, low-fat, and whole-milk products.

Egg whites can be used in muffins if you wish to omit the cholesterol in the yolks. You do lose some taste and richness in texture, but the sacrifice is minor if it is important for you to watch your cholesterol.

---

### equipment

Just as quality ingredients give a quality product, quality equipment makes baking a pleasure. Why go to all the bother, then sabotage your efforts with a frustrating tool or the wrong pan? Sometimes we collect equipment on sale, or someone gives us something special. I find my plain old aluminum cake pans give the highest, tenderest cake layers of all. While I appreciate the ease of cleaning nonstick pans, I find that the texture of muffins and fruit breads is tougher when baked in them than when baked in Pyrex or aluminum pans. Try it yourself: Borrow a different kind of pan and compare your results before you buy more pans. You need

i knew you were coming so i baked a
**cake**

pans that brown well but do not result in tough crusts on what should be tender cakes. Invest in good equipment and your equipment will take good care of you.

As I worked on this book, one piece of equipment truly surprised and delighted me. It was not "European," "Gourmet," or "Deluxe Super-Duper," it was my *two-cup Pyrex glass measuring cup!* It goes into the microwave to boil water, melt chocolate, or make puddings. If I add ingredients in the right sequence, I can measure all my liquids into the one cup, blend gently, and then easily pour them into any batter working in my mixer. Then a quick rinse or into the dishwasher. I bought myself a second one.

Other favorite tools are a *curved rubber spatula* and *bowls that open out* sufficiently for easy mixing without worrying that everything in the bowl will travel over the sides, or that the bowl is so deep that combining everything evenly from the bottom will take a super effort. Basically, I want my tools to work with me, not fight me.

Here's what you'll need to bake your way through this book. All these items are readily available at supermarkets, housewares departments, or even hardware stores:

Measuring spoons
Dry measuring cups
1-cup, 2-cup, and 1-quart Pyrex measuring cups
½-cup Pyrex glass bowls
2-quart microwavable bowl
Rubber spatula (I find one with a curved blade is most useful)
Offset metal spatulas, 4-inch and 8-inch
2-quart saucepan
1-, 2-, and 3-quart mixing bowls
Electric mixer
Food processor
9x4 loaf pan
8-inch square Pyrex pan
9x13 baking pan
Two 8- or 9-inch round cake pans
9-inch pie pans
9-inch tart shells
6-cup bundt or tube pan
9-inch springform pan

Two cookie sheets, aluminum or nonstick

8-inch nonstick sauté pan

Roasting pan

Knives, one small paring and one large chef's chopping knife

Cutting board

3-inch biscuit cutters

Box or handheld grater

Mixing spoons

Can opener

Strainer

Oven mitts

Apple corer

Vegetable peeler

Airtight containers to hold your products

Zip-top bags, 1-quart and 1-gallon sizes

Toothpicks

Aluminum foil, plastic wrap, and wax paper

Cupcake and petit-four paper cups

Optional: kitchen shears; gratin (oval baking dish) to go from oven to table; cookie cutters in various shapes; minimuffin tins; miniloaf pans; pastry brush; coeur à la crème mold; piping bags and tips; 3-inch tart pans; cheesecloth; 1-inch melon baller; juicer; blender; baking parchment paper

## the microwave

While the smells wafting from buttery treats baking in the oven just can't be beat, a microwave oven can speed up dessert just as an electric mixer or food processor can. It's a great time-saving tool if used properly for those items it does best, such as puddings, some confections, and melting chocolate and butter.

i knew you were coming so i baked a cake

chapter one

# classic
# cakes

butter cake
boston cream pie
"don't do it" chocolate cake
anita farber's banana cake
gingerbread
mango-molasses upside-down cake
cheesecake
smooth as a baby's . . . carrot cake
almond torte

If you can produce the cakes in this chapter, your reputation as a good baker is guaranteed. These are cakes to be eaten, not just admired. The recipes are standards you can adapt, vary, and shape as your own. As you make these cakes over and over, they will become yours. With different icings, slight variations, and personal touches, this list should get you through almost any event or celebration required of good home bakers.

## time savers

- Measure and combine the dry ingredients the day before baking and store them in a zip-top bag.
- An hour before you're going to bake, set out the eggs, butter, and milk or sour cream to come to room temperature, and go on to other tasks. If you don't do this, measure the butter and the sour cream or milk into separate glass bowls or Pyrex cups. Place them in the microwave on the lowest setting for one minute. Touch to see if they are approximating room temperature.
- Use cooking spray. It really helps to release cakes quickly, and you don't have to remember that extra teaspoon of butter in addition to the amount listed in the ingredients.
- Many of these cakes, such as **Butter Cake, "Don't Do It" Chocolate Cake,** Anita Farber's Banana Cake, and Smooth as a Baby's . . . Carrot Cake, can be baked in cupcake tins. A one-layer recipe makes approximately twelve cup-cakes; a two-layer recipe makes approximately twenty-four cupcakes. Decrease the baking time by about 10 minutes.

classic
cakes

# butter cake

**Makes two 8- or 9-inch rounds, 24 cupcakes, or 1 9x13 sheet cake**

Cooking spray (optional)

½ pound (2 sticks) unsalted butter

1 ½ cups sugar

3 eggs, slightly beaten

2 teaspoons vanilla extract

2½ cups flour, sifted, or 3 cups cake flour (omit the cornstarch if using cake flour)

¼ cup cornstarch (if using all-purpose flour)

1 tablespoon baking powder

¼ teaspoon salt

1 cup milk

**EQUIPMENT**
electric mixer or food processor; 2-quart mixing bowl; curved rubber spatula; two 8- or 9-inch cake pans, muffin tins and paper cups, or 9x13 cake pan; wax paper; serving plate

*T*his cake works in a remarkable number of ways. It happily conforms to different cake pans, loves to become cupcakes, holds up to blueberries, and can become a Boston cream pie or a birthday cake. It can even be mixed in a food processor. It freezes well, it's sweet enough to be served without icing but adapts well to many flavors of buttercream, and it can be paired with the **"Don't Do It" Chocolate Cake** (page 33) for a sky-high creation when you really want to put on the Ritz. What more could you ask of one recipe?

1. Preheat the oven to 350°F. Butter or spray the cake pans and coat each pan with 1 teaspoon of flour.

**USING AN ELECTRIC MIXER:**

2. Cream the butter and incorporate the sugar, beating slowly for 2 minutes until smooth.
3. Add the eggs and the vanilla extract and beat 2 minutes more.
4. Combine the flour, cornstarch (if using), baking powder, and salt in the mixing bowl. Starting and ending with the flour, alternate flour and milk additions, scraping down the sides of the mixing bowl two or three times, until the batter is smooth.
5. Spread the batter evenly in the prepared cake pans.
6. Bake about 30 to 35 minutes, until golden on top and springy to the touch; a toothpick inserted in the middle should come out clean. Don't overbake. Bake cupcakes about 20 minutes.
7. Allow the layers to cool 10 minutes in their pans, then tap along the edges to loosen. Nudge the layers out of their pans onto wax paper so the bottoms cool before you ice them. When you are ready to ice, tear wax paper into strips to tuck under the cake edges to protect the serving plate. Choose any favorite icing; they all go with this cake.

**USING A FOOD PROCESSOR:**

1. Cut the butter into 8 pieces directly into the bowl of the food processor, add the sugar, and process until evenly combined, about 30 seconds.

i knew you were coming so i baked a **cake**

2. Add the eggs and vanilla, pulsing until fully incorporated.
3. Combine the flour, cornstarch (if using), baking powder, and salt in a mixing bowl. Add half of the dry mixture and pulse 4 to 6 times, just to blend.
4. Add the milk and pulse to blend.
5. Add the rest of the flour mix and pulse briefly.
6. Finish stirring the batter with a rubber spatula until it is smooth.
7. Continue the recipe starting with Step 5.

### VARIATIONS:

**lemon cake**   Add 1 teaspoon lemon zest with the vanilla extract for a lemon cake. Use a **Fruit Purée** (pages 176–79) or **Lemon Curd** (page 156) between the layers, and finish with Lemon or Orange Juice Glaze (pages 61 and 62.)

**almond butter cake**   Substitute 1 teaspoon almond extract for the vanilla. Frost with Nutella or with chocolate- or praline-flavored **Buttercream** (page 63).

**orange cake**   Substitute 6 ounces orange juice concentrate, thawed, and 2 ounces water for the milk, and use 1 teaspoon orange zest in the batter. Put **Lemon Curd** (page 156) between the layers and confectioners' sugar on top. Garnish with summer berries.

## Basic Points About Butter Cakes

• **Plain butter cakes are much more finicky than chocolate cakes.**

• **Because of the more delicate balance of butterfats and flavor, I recommend using only the best butter and pure vanilla extract.**

• **You must be very careful in timing the baking in order to achieve a moist and delicate texture.**

• **You must be sure all your ingredients start at room temperature so they will incorporate smoothly, leaving no gummy spots.**

• **Butter or use cooking spray in your cake pan and don't forget to flour it for easy release when the cake is done. You can take great pride in a really good Butter Cake!**

classic cakes

# boston cream pie

**Makes 10 to 12 servings**

EQUIPMENT
8-inch offset spatula;
toothpicks; wax paper;
serving plate

*T*his classic pie gets assembled and chilled before serving, but because each element can be made well ahead of time, I think you'll find time to enjoy it.

**DO AHEAD:**

1. Make the **Butter Cake** (page 30) in two 9-inch cake pans.
2. Make a double recipe of the **Vanilla Pudding** (page 143).
3. Make the Chocolate Glaze (page 127).

**TO ASSEMBLE:**

4. Set one cake layer on a serving plate.
5. Cut four 3-inch-wide strips of wax paper and gently raise the edges of the cake layer with a spatula. Tuck the wax paper under the cake to protect the serving plate from drips.
6. Pour the Vanilla Pudding onto the center of the cake layer and spread evenly to the edges.
7. Carefully place the second cake layer on top of the pudding. If you have time, you can poke 3 or 4 toothpicks through the top layer and the pudding into the lower layer and chill for about 1 hour to firm the pudding. Be sure to remove the toothpicks before you ice the cake.
8. Warm the Chocolate Glaze and stir until it will pour readily. (You may need to add ¼ cup more milk or cream to thin it.) Starting in the center, pour the glaze in a spiral outward to the top edge of the cake layer. Use a spatula to even out the top and push some of the icing to the edge. Chill at least 30 minutes before serving.

i knew you
were coming
so i baked a
cake

# "don't do it" chocolate cake

**Makes two 8- or 9-inch cake layers, one 9x13 sheet cake, or about 24 cupcakes**

*T*his is the Don't Do It cake. Don't melt the chocolate. Don't soften the butter. Don't sift the flour. Don't beat it for more than two minutes. Don't use more than one bowl. Don't spend more than ten minutes putting this cake together. While other cocoa powders work fine with this recipe, I think it is best with Hershey's.

Cooking spray (optional)

¾ cup cocoa powder

2 cups sugar

1¾ cups flour

1 teaspoon salt

1½ teaspoons baking soda

1½ teaspoons baking powder

1 cup milk

½ cup vegetable oil

2 eggs

2 teaspoons vanilla extract

**EQUIPMENT**
1-quart Pyrex cup; electric mixer; rubber spatula; 8- or 9-inch cake pan, muffin tin and paper cups, or 9x13 cake pan

1. Preheat the oven to 350°F. Grease and flour the pan or pans, or line the muffin tins with paper cups.
2. Measure the cocoa, sugar, flour, salt, baking soda, and baking powder into the bowl of the electric mixer and allow the mixer to combine them for 10 to 15 seconds. Measure the milk, oil, eggs, and vanilla together into the Pyrex cup, turn off the machine, and then add this to the mixed dry ingredients. Beat on medium speed *2 minutes only.*
3. Bring 1 cup water to a boil in the Pyrex cup by microwaving on high power for about 2 minutes (or boil water in your teakettle and measure 1 cup).
4. Remove the bowl with the batter from the mixer and stir in the boiling water by hand with the spatula. Pour the batter into the prepared pan, pans, or muffin tins.
5. Bake 30 to 35 minutes for rounds, 35 to 40 minutes for a rectangular pan, or 15 to 20 minutes for cupcakes, or until a toothpick inserted in the center comes out clean and the cake center springs back when you touch it.
6. Let cook in the pans 10 minutes, remove to cake racks, and let cool completely before icing.
7. Frost with Chocolate Sour Cream Icing (page 65), **Chocolate Cream Cheese Icing** (page 64), or your choice of **Flavored Buttercream,** or turn it into a Black Forest Cake (page 194).

classic cakes

# anita farber's banana cake

**Makes one 9x4 loaf, one 8- or 9-inch cake layer, or 12 cupcakes (doubled, one 9x13 sheet cake or two 8- or 9-inch cake layers)**

Cooking spray (optional)

½ cup vegetable oil

¼ cup plus 1 tablespoon sour cream, yogurt, or buttermilk

3 very ripe bananas, roughly mashed

2 eggs

1 teaspoon vanilla extract

1¾ cups flour

1 cup sugar

1 teaspoon baking soda

½ teaspoon salt

1 cup chopped walnuts (optional)

### EQUIPMENT
3-quart mixing bowl; 1-quart Pyrex cup; mixing spoon; one 9x4-inch loaf pan, one 8- or 9-inch cake pan, or muffin tin and paper cups

*This recipe can be doubled or quadrupled if you need sheet cakes for the masses. It is moist and keeps wonderfully for days in the refrigerator, or several weeks in the freezer. Start hoarding those too, too ripe bananas in the freezer for this one.*

1. Preheat the oven to 350°F.
2. Use 1 tablespoon of the oil, or the cooking spray, to generously coat the bottom and sides of your baking pan.
3. Measure and combine the oil, sour cream, bananas, eggs, and vanilla in a 1-quart Pyrex cup.
4. Measure and combine the flour, sugar, baking soda, and salt in the mixing bowl.
5. Add the wet ingredients to the dry and stir. Add the walnuts if you wish.
6. Pour the batter into the pan and bake about 45 minutes. Cupcakes bake in 25 to 30 minutes. The cake will take on a rich, dark brown color and spring back when you touch it lightly, and a toothpick inserted in the center will come out clean.

**QUICK TIP:** Measure dry ingredients into a zip-top bag and label it for when you will bake next.

i knew you were coming so i baked a cake

# gingerbread

**Makes one 8- or 9-inch round or 8-inch square cake, serving 6 to 8**

*T*he warm, spicy aromas of ginger and molasses say homemade America to me. I like this best warm from the oven. Serve it with peach or mango ice cream, **Gingered Whipped Cream** (page 71), or **Lemon Curd** (page 156), or simply garnish it with chopped crystallized ginger and a sprinkle of confectioners' sugar.

1. Preheat the oven to 350°F, and butter or use cooking spray on the bottom and sides of the pan.
2. Cream the butter with the sugar; add the egg, molasses, and ⅓ cup boiling water.
3. Add the dry ingredients and mix just until blended.
4. Pour into the cake pan and bake about 30 minutes, or until a toothpick inserted in the center comes out clean.
5. Let cool 10 minutes, then run a knife around the inside of the pan to release the gingerbread. Invert a serving plate over the pan and let the cake drop onto the plate. Garnish with crystallized ginger if you wish.

Cooking spray (optional)

2 ounces (½ stick) unsalted butter

⅓ cup sugar

I egg

⅓ cup molasses

I ¼ cups flour

I teaspoon baking soda

½ teaspoon salt

I teaspoon ground ginger

Chopped crystallized ginger for garnish (optional)

**EQUIPMENT**

electric mixer, or 3-quart mixing bowl and mixing spoon; I-quart Pyrex cup; curved rubber spatula; 8- or 9-inch round or 8-inch square cake pan; serving plate

classic cakes

# mango-molasses upside-down cake

**Makes one 9-inch cake layer**

2 ounces (½ stick) unsalted butter

⅓ cup dark brown sugar

I mango or 2 green apples, peeled, cored, and sliced

I recipe Gingerbread (page 35)

Chopped crystallized ginger, for garnish

**EQUIPMENT**
9-inch cake pan; knife; serving plate; rubber spatula

*H*ere is an upside-down cake that's fragrant, fruity, and unusual.

1. Preheat the oven to 350°F.
2. Melt the butter in the cake pan as the oven is warming up.
3. Add the sugar and stir to dissolve.
4. Layer the fruit slices evenly in the cake pan, fanning them around in a pinwheel.
5. Carefully pour the gingerbread batter onto the fruit and bake about 30 minutes.
6. Cool 10 minutes, then run a knife around the inside of the pan to loosen the sides. Invert a serving plate over the pan and let the cake drop onto the serving plate. If any of the fruit clings to the pan, use a spatula to free it and smooth it onto the cake, fitting it into the pinwheel pattern.
7. Serve garnished with the crystallized ginger.

i knew you were coming so i baked a **cake**

# cheesecake

**Makes one 8- or 9-inch cheesecake, a 9-inch pie, or a 9x13 pan of bar cookies**

*I ate a lot of cheesecake as a young woman. In my middle years, I find it sticks to my middle, but I still love the mild taste and creamy texture, and I always look at cheesecakes when I pass a bakery or a dessert display counter. Here are two sizes—one for a springform pan, and a reduced recipe for a pie size, which also works as bar cookies. If your cheesecake cracks in settling as it cools, you can cover it with a* **Berry Purée** *or Strawberries in Orange Liqueur (page 167) or a Jam Glaze (page 60).*

**MAKE THE CRUST:**

1. Preheat the oven to 325°F.
2. Add the sugar and cinnamon to the graham crackers in a zip-top bag. Crush with a rolling pin to make 1¾ cups sweetened crumbs.
3. Melt the butter in the Pyrex cup in the microwave for 1 minute on Medium.
4. Pour the butter into the bag with the crumbs and mix together. Transfer the crumbs into the pan, and with your hands, pat this onto the sides and bottom.
5. Bake for 10 minutes.
6. Remove the crust from the oven and set aside to cool.
7. Set a roasting pan filled with 1 inch of water on the lower shelf and adjust the upper shelf to the middle of the oven, just above the pan of water, while you prepare the filling.

**MAKE THE CHEESECAKE FILLING:**

1. Beat the cream cheese in the electric mixer to soften it.
2. Add the eggs, one at a time, and scrape down the sides of the mixing bowl to incorporate them thoroughly.
3. Add the sour cream and blend well.
4. Add the sugar, then the vanilla—and the optional lemon zest. Slowly sprinkle in the optional flour and mix just until blended.
5. Pour the filling into the crust, smooth the top, and set the pan on the uppermost oven shelf to bake for about 1 hour. Check with a gentle shake

**crust for 8- or 9-inch springform pan or 9-inch pie:**

*¼ cup sugar and 1 teaspoon cinnamon or ¼ cup Cinnamon-Sugar (page 22)*

*1 package (about 5 ounces) graham crackers or ⅓ package (approximately 4½ ounces or 1½ cups) prepared graham cracker crumbs*

*¼ pound (1 stick) unsalted butter*

**filling for 8- or 9-inch springform pan:**

*2 pounds cream cheese*

*3 eggs*

*1 cup sour cream*

*1 cup sugar*

*1 teaspoon vanilla extract*

*Grated zest of 1 lemon (½ teaspoon) (optional)*

*2 tablespoons flour to make the cheesecake more stable (optional)*

**EQUIPMENT**
zip-top bag; rolling pin; 1-cup Pyrex cup; baking pan of your choice; electric mixer; curved spatula; roasting pan

classic cakes

to see if the center has firmed or is still wobbly. (The cake will settle some as it cools, and wobbly will become creamy when it is chilled and served. If you can cool it gradually, leaving it in an open, turned-off oven, and if you run a knife around the inside of the pan, releasing the cake from the sides, it is less likely to crack on top.)

**filling for 9-inch pie or 9x13-inch pan of bar cookies:**

*1 pound cream cheese*

*2 eggs*

*½ cup sugar*

*½ teaspoon vanilla extract*

*Juice and/or zest of one lemon (about 1 ounce juice and ½ teaspoon zest) (optional)*

**EQUIPMENT**

electric mixer; rubber spatula

## VARIATION:

1. Preheat the oven to 350°F.
2. Make the crust as directed above. Press it into the baking pan. Bake for 10 minutes. Remove from the oven and let cool.
3. Beat the cream cheese in the electric mixer until softened. Add the eggs and beat until incorporated. Add the sugar, vanilla, optional lemon juice and zest and beat until smooth. Pour the filling into the prepared crust.
4. Bake for 30 minutes until the filling is puffed and the top begins to take on color.
5. Let cool completely before cutting.

**QUICK TIP:** Grind up the whole box of graham crackers with ¾ cup sugar and 3 teaspoons cinnamon in the food processor. Store the extra in a plastic container in the refrigerator and you are halfway to two more cheesecakes!

i knew you were coming so i baked a **cake**

# smooth as a baby's . . . carrot cake

**Makes one 8- or 9-inch layer, or 8-inch square, or 12 cupcakes**

*O*kay, okay, laugh at the main ingredient, but if you don't have to grate the carrots and you could hold the raisins and nuts to put in the cream cheese icing, won't you try a quick carrot cake? It doubles well to fill a 9x13 pan or two 8- or 9-inch rounds. It's as quick as a muffin mix, and you can bake the layers a day ahead. Add goodies to the cream cheese icing to finish it the next.

1. Preheat the oven to 350°F. Grease the pan with cooking spray or wipe 1 tablespoon oil around the inside, or set paper liners in the muffin cups.
2. Measure the flour, brown sugar, baking soda, baking powder, cinnamon, and salt into the mixing bowl and stir to distribute evenly. Measure the oil, carrots, vanilla, and egg directly onto the dry ingredients and stir to incorporate, leaving no lumps. Add any optional ingredients to the batter or save them to mix into the icing.
3. Bake 25 to 30 minutes for a cake or 20 to 25 minutes for cupcakes. The cake is done when a toothpick inserted in the center comes out clean. Let cool in the pan 10 minutes, then run a knife around the inside of the pan to loosen the cake. Place a serving plate over the pan and invert, letting the cake drop onto the plate. Cool completely before icing.

**FINISHING TOUCHES:**

4. If you have reserved the optional additions, garnish the outer edges of the iced cake with your choice of raisins, nuts, and/or toasted coconut. Chill at least 1 hour to set the icing before serving.

**NOTE:** If you really can't bring yourself to shop the babyfood aisle, buy a bag of frozen carrots. Whiz them, still frozen, in the food processor, measure 1½ cups packed chopped carrots (10 to 12 ounces), reduce the flour to 1½ cups, and proceed.

Cooking spray (optional)

1¾ cups flour

1 cup dark brown sugar

1 teaspoon baking soda

1 teaspoon baking powder

1½ teaspoon cinnamon

½ teaspoon salt

¼ cup canola or other vegetable oil

1 cup baby food carrot or sweet potato purée

1 teaspoon vanilla extract

2 eggs, slightly beaten

1 recipe Cream Cheese Icing (page 64) (optional)

1 cup coconut, ½ cup walnuts, ½ cup raisins (optional)

**EQUIPMENT**
8-inch square baking pan, or 12-cup muffin tin and paper cups, or 8- or 9-inch round cake pan; 3-quart mixing bowl, mixing spoon

classic cakes

39

# almond torte

**Makes one 9-inch layer baked in a cake pan or springform pan**

*It takes just a few minutes to measure this into the food processor, zest one lemon, and beat the egg whites. The cake layers combine very well with many different flavors and can become many different tortes. See how many variations you can devise. (The one layer may be used as is or sliced horizontally for two layers.)*

*Cooking spray (optional)*

*2 cups (about 7 ounces) whole almonds*

*1 ⅓ cups sugar*

*½ teaspoon salt*

*½ cup flour*

*Zest of 1 lemon (about ½ teaspoon) (squeeze the lemon and freeze the juice for another use) or 1 ½ teaspoons minced dried lemon zest*

*8 egg whites*

## EQUIPMENT
food processor, electric mixer, or 3-quart mixing bowl and whisk; 9-inch springform pan or 9-inch cake pan lined with wax paper or baking parchment; grater; mixing bowl; curved rubber spatula; knife

1. Preheat the oven to 325°F and grease or spray the pan.
2. Grind the almonds with the sugar and salt in the food processor to a very fine consistency.
3. Measure the flour and zest the lemon directly into the processor and pulse 2 or 3 times to combine with the nuts and sugar.
4. Whip the egg whites until stiff peaks stand on their own.
5. Gently fold the nut mixture into the egg whites, one-third at a time. When it is thoroughly blended, pour the batter into the pan and shake it gently to settle.
6. Bake in the middle of the oven about 1 hour. A toothpick inserted in the center will come out clean when the torte is done; the top will be golden and firm to the touch.
7. Allow the torte to cool in the pan 10 minutes, then run the knife around the edge to loosen and turn onto a plate to cool completely before finishing (or loosen the sides of the springform pan and gently remove the torte).

**NOTES:**

· Use up the yolks in **Lemon Curd** (page 156) or in **Vanilla** or **Rice Pudding** (pages 145 and 143).

**VARIATIONS:**

· Hazelnuts work as well as almonds.
· If you can purchase ground nuts, mix the dry ingredients (including the ground nuts) together and fold into the egg whites—faster still!
· Substitute ¼ cup cocoa powder for ¼ cup of the flour and omit the lemon zest for a chocolate torte.

i knew you were coming so i baked a cake

**FINISHING TOUCHES:**

· Dress up one layer with a sprinkling of confectioners' sugar.
· Try Chocolate Sour Cream Icing (page 65).
· Slice horizontally through the cake to make two layers and fill with 1 cup of **Whipped Cream** (page 68), Chocolate Whipped Cream (page 70), raspberry jam, **Dried Apricot Purée or Prune Purée** (pages 178, 179), **Mocha** or **Chocolate Buttercream** (page 63), **Lemon Curd** (page 156), Nutella, or Dulce de Leche (page 75).

classic
cakes

chapter two

# coffee cakes, quick breads, muffins, brownies, blondies, and crêpes

sour cream coffee cake
apple kuchen
upside-down berry cake
date-nut fruit bread
mom's blueberry muffins
strawberry yogurt muffins
microwave brownies
blondies in a pot
crêpes
crêpe fillings

In my family, for nighttime "milk and cookies," tea in the afternoon, or just plain snacking, the preferred treats are coffee cakes, quick breads, and muffins with lots of fruit. These recipes are also handy additions to lunchboxes, and the perfect offering for unexpected guests.

# sour cream coffee cake

**Makes one 6-cup bundt or tube pan**

*H*ere *is an adaptation of my mom's classic, without the electric mixer, without waiting for the butter to soften, and without alternating additions.*

1. Preheat the oven to 350°F, and spray or grease the baking pan.
2. Melt the butter in the saucepan.
3. Remove from the heat and add the sugar, vanilla, salt, and sour cream. Stir to combine. Add the flour, baking soda, and baking powder. Stir to combine. Add the eggs, break them up with the fork, and mix in thoroughly.
4. Spoon half the batter into the prepared pan. Layer in the optional fruit or nuts and half the cinnamon-sugar. Pour in the rest of the batter. Top with the remaining cinnamon-sugar.
5. Bake 45 to 55 minutes, just until the top takes on some color. When a toothpick inserted in the center comes out dry, the cake is done. Allow to cool 10 minutes, then set a serving plate over the pan, invert, and allow the cake to drop onto the plate. A soft sprinkle of confectioners' sugar just before serving will embellish the cake.

**VARIATIONS:**

Try these flavorings and fruits to create a range of moist, delicious possibilities.

- Substitute ½ teaspoon almond extract for the vanilla and sprinkle ½ cup sliced almonds on top. (For this presentation, serve the cake right side up.)
- Add the zest of 1 lemon or 2 oranges to the batter.
- Try half a cup of dried cherries, 1 cup cherry jam, or 1 cup canned or frozen cherries, chopped and strained, swirled into the batter.
- Layer 1 cup cranberry sauce mixed with 2 teaspoons orange zest onto half the batter, then fill with the remaining batter.
- Spread 1 cup of **Oatmeal Pecan Crisp** (page 66) topping on the top of the cake for a right-side-up crunchy finish.

Cooking spray (optional)

¼ pound (1 stick) unsalted butter

1 cup sugar

1 teaspoon vanilla extract

½ teaspoon salt

1 cup sour cream or yogurt

2 cups flour, sifted, or 2 level measured cups with 2 rounded tablespoons removed

1 teaspoon baking soda

1 teaspoon baking powder

3 eggs

¼ cup Cinnamon-Sugar (page 22) or Mixed Spices (page 22)

Dried fruit and/or chopped nuts, and confectioners' sugar for garnish (optional; see additional suggestions at end of recipe)

**EQUIPMENT**

2-quart saucepan; mixing spoon; fork; 6-cup tube or bundt baking pan; serving plate

coffee cakes, quick breads, muffins, brownies, blondies, and crêpes

# apple kuchen

**Makes one 9-inch layer baked in a springform, or a 9x13-inch cake pan**

Cooking spray (optional)

¼ pound (1 stick) unsalted butter

1 cup sugar

½ teaspoon vanilla extract

¼ teaspoon salt

¼ cup milk

1 ½ cups flour, or 2 cups cake flour (omit the cornstarch if using cake flour)

¼ cup cornstarch (if using all-purpose flour)

2 teaspoons baking powder

2 eggs

3 to 4 cups sliced tart apples such as greenings (2 large), peeled and sliced ¼ inch thick

¼ cup Cinnamon-Sugar (page 22)

**EQUIPMENT**
2-quart saucepan; rubber spatula; 9-inch springform pan, or 9x13-inch pan

*T*his kind of fruit-topped cake has a long history in European kitchens. It has great keeping qualities and is wonderful served warm with morning coffee, for brunch, or reheated with late afternoon tea. To me, this is the *cake that truly says "homemade."* This cake doesn't mind what size pan you bake it in, or if you want to reheat it; just be generous with the fruit and the cinnamon-sugar on top. In the summer, try this with peaches, plums, and/or blueberries.

1. Preheat the oven to 350°F. Grease the baking pan with melted butter or cooking spray.
2. Melt the butter in the saucepan.
3. Add the sugar, vanilla, salt, and milk, and stir until smooth. Add the flour, cornstarch, and baking powder, mixing just until the batter is smooth. Add the eggs and mix thoroughly.
4. Pour the batter into the baking pan and level the surface.
5. Layer the apples on top, overlapping the slices.
6. Generously sprinkle with cinnamon-sugar and bake for about 50 to 60 minutes, depending on the pan's shape. A toothpick inserted in the center will come out clean when the cake is done. Place on a wire rack to cool. Then loosen the edges of the springform pan and remove the cake. (If you use a 9x13 pan, serve in the pan.)

i knew you were coming so i baked a **cake**

# upside-down berry cake

**Makes one 9-inch cake**

Since it holds up so well with fruit on the top, I tried the kuchen batter with fruit on the bottom. It makes a terrific upside-down cake with lots of yummy sauce already on top. It's great—it always comes out of the pan intact!

1. Preheat the oven to 350°F.
2. Melt the butter in the cake pan as the oven is warming.
3. Wash and pick over fresh berries and drain well. Toss the berries with the sugar to coat, and add the optional lemon juice and zest.
4. Remove the cake pan from the oven and swirl the butter all around to coat the pan bottom and sides.
5. Pour the berries into the cake pan and shake into a level layer.
6. Prepare the Kuchen and pour it over the berries.
7. Bake about 40 to 45 minutes. The cake is done when the top is browned and a toothpick inserted in the middle comes out dry.
8. Let cool in the pan 5 minutes. You will see the cake shrinking away from the sides of the pan.
9. Run a knife around the sides of the cake if any edge does stick, and invert onto your serving plate. (Be sure there is a lip on the plate or an extra inch around the rim to hold any sauce that slides off the cake.) Don't rush this step. Allow gravity to pull the berries and sauce onto your cake about 5 minutes before you try to remove the pan and then, using the knife, tip up one edge and gently lift the pan off.

**VARIATIONS:**

· Substitute one bag of fresh or frozen cranberries, or a 15-ounce can of whole-berry cranberry sauce, for the blueberries. To fresh or frozen cranberries, washed and picked over, add 1½ cups sugar and the zest of 1 orange. Use the cranberry sauce as is. Proceed with the directions.

· Canned fruits, such as apricots, peaches, even fruit cocktail, can all become upside-down cakes. Strain off the juice and add the fruit to the melted butter in the pan; no extra sugar is needed. Pour the cake batter on top and proceed to bake.

2 ounces (½ stick) unsalted butter

1 pint fresh blueberries or one 12-ounce bag frozen blueberries

½ cup sugar

Zest and juice of 1 lemon (optional), about ½ teaspoon and 1 ounce, respectively

1 recipe Kuchen batter (page 46)

**EQUIPMENT**
9-inch cake pan; 2-quart saucepan; curved rubber spatula; knife; serving plate

coffee cakes, quick breads, muffins, brownies, blondies, and crêpes

# date-nut fruit bread

**Makes one 6-cup tube pan, one 9x4-inch loaf, eight 3x5-inch miniloaves, or 12 muffins**

*Cooking spray or muffin cup papers (optional)*

*1 cup chopped dates*

*1 cup coarsely chopped walnuts*

*1 teaspoon baking soda*

*1 teaspoon baking powder*

*½ teaspoon salt*

*3 tablespoons unsalted butter*

*2 eggs*

*1 cup sugar*

*1 teaspoon vanilla extract*

*1½ cups flour*

## EQUIPMENT

1-quart and 3-quart mixing bowls; 1-quart Pyrex cup; mixing spoon; 6-cup tube pan, 9x4-inch loaf pan, eight 3x5-inch miniloaf pans, or 12-cup muffin tin and paper cups

*T*his classic combination works in all kinds of shapes, and it takes nicely to some **Lemon Curd** (page 156) or **Gingered Whipped Cream** (page 71) moistening each slice. Try it with some Orange Juice Glaze (page 62) glistening on top.

1. Preheat the oven to 350°F. Butter or spray your baking pan generously, or line the muffin tins with the paper cups.
2. Measure the dates, walnuts, baking soda, baking powder, salt, and butter into the 1-quart mixing bowl.
3. Bring ¾ cup water to a boil (about 2 minutes in the microwave on High) and pour it over the date mixture. Let stand for 15 to 20 minutes.
4. In the 3-quart mixing bowl, measure and mix together the eggs, sugar, vanilla, and flour. Add the date mixture to the egg mixture. Combine well and pour into your prepared baking pan(s).
5. Bake for 45 to 60 minutes for the tube pan and the large loaf, 30 to 35 minutes for the miniloaves, and 20 to 25 minutes for the muffins. The cake is done when a toothpick inserted in the center comes out dry. Invert the serving plate onto the cake and flip upside down, allowing the cake to drop onto the plate. Glaze when cool, if desired.

i knew you were coming so i baked a **cake**

48

# mom's blueberry muffins

**Makes 24 muffins**

*T*his is my mom's recipe, and it's superb. Everyone reaches for these muffins first. They are very soft, cakelike, and fruity without being supersweet. They freeze well and kids really love them.

1. Preheat the oven to 350°F.
2. Using an electric mixer, cream the butter and incorporate the sugar in the 3-quart bowl, beating slowly for 2 minutes until smooth. (If mixing by hand, beat 3 or 4 minutes to ensure a smooth mixture.) Add the eggs and the vanilla and beat about 2 minutes more.
3. Measure and combine the flour and baking powder in a 1-quart bowl. Measure the milk.
4. Starting and ending with the flour mixture, add the dry ingredients and milk alternately to the butter mixture, scraping down the sides of the bowl two or three times.
5. When the batter is smooth, remove from the mixer, spoon it into the paper-lined muffin cups, and drop in the blueberries by hand.
6. Bake for 20 to 25 minutes until lightly colored; a toothpick inserted in the middle of a muffin should come out clean.

¼ pound (1 stick) unsalted butter

1 cup sugar

2 eggs, slightly beaten

1 teaspoon vanilla extract

1 cup milk

2 cups flour, sifted, or 2 level measured cups with 2 rounded tablespoons removed

1 rounded tablespoon baking powder

1 pint blueberries

**EQUIPMENT**
electric mixer or 3-quart mixing bowl, 1-quart mixing bowl, and mixing spoon; 1-cup Pyrex cup; tablespoon; curved rubber spatula; two 12-cup muffin tins and paper cups

**NOTE:** Fresh berries do make the best muffins, but if you use frozen berries, one 12-ounce bag is enough. If the berries thaw out, they give off a lot of their juice and flavor, so I try to use them unthawed. Toss 1 tablespoon of flour into the frozen berries in the bag and stir them around before adding the berries to the muffins. The flour dredging will prevent their sinking to the bottom.

If you want to use dry blueberries, reconstitute them by warming about 1 cup of berries in 2 cups of water. Microwave 2 minutes on High, or pour on boiling water and allow the berries to steep about 5 minutes. Drain off the water and add the berries to the muffin batter.

**VARIATIONS:** For a light orange muffin, substitute 6 ounces of orange juice concentrate and 2 ounces of water for the milk and add the zest of 1 orange. You may also substitute 1½ cups fresh cranberries or 1 cup dry cranberries. Orange Juice Glaze (page 62) finishes these muffins beautifully.

coffee cakes, quick breads, muffins, brownies, blondies, and crêpes

49

# strawberry yogurt muffins

**Makes 12 muffins**

1 cup flour

1½ teaspoons baking
powder

¼ teaspoon salt

½ cup sugar

¼ pound (1 stick) unsalted
butter

1 egg

1½ teaspoons vanilla ex-
tract

½ cup strawberry yogurt

1 mashed banana

½ cup chopped strawber-
ries (optional)

**EQUIPMENT**
one 12-cup muffin tin and
paper cups; 1-cup Pyrex
cup; 3-quart mixing bowl;
curved rubber spatula

*I* came into the kitchen one morning planning to bake some quick muffins. I found a ripe (or rotting, depending on whether you share my son's opinion) banana, and strawberry yogurt (William's favorite). So here's a recipe you might use with flavored yogurt. It's a delicate muffin, and 2 dozen are as easy to make as 1 dozen, so double the recipe if you like. Freeze extras for a quickly warmed brunch treat or afternoon snack.

1. Preheat the oven to 350°F.
2. In the mixing bowl, combine the flour, baking powder, salt, and sugar.
3. Melt the butter in a Pyrex cup in the microwave, 30 seconds on High (another 15 seconds if needed), and add it to the dry ingredients. Add the egg, vanilla, yogurt, banana, and optional berries, mixing just to incorporate.
4. When blended, spoon into lined muffin cups and bake 20 to 25 minutes.

**VARIATION:** You can substitute blueberry, cherry, or peach yogurt.

**NOTE:** Many of the Classic Cakes—such as the **Butter Cake, "Don't Do It" Chocolate Cake, Anita Farber's Banana Cake,** and Smooth as a Baby's . . . Carrot Cake—can also become muffins, with 10 minutes' less baking time.

i knew you
were coming
so i baked a
cake

# microwave brownies

**Makes nine 3-inch squares or sixteen 2-inch brownies**

*I*f you need the smell of brownies baking in your oven, you can do it in 30 to 40 minutes. But when you're really rushed, try these brownies done in the microwave for real, homemade treats in less than 10 minutes with no pan to scrub.

1. Line the pan with wax paper, using enough to come up the sides.
2. Melt the butter and chocolate on Medium for 1½ minutes in the Pyrex cup in the microwave. (You can continue heating the butter and chocolate 15 seconds at a time if they don't melt as you stir them together.) If you are using premelted chocolate, just heat the butter 1 minute, then stir in the chocolate.
3. Add the sugar to the cup and mix thoroughly.
4. Add the eggs, vanilla, and salt and mix thoroughly.
5. Stir in the flour until it is just incorporated, and then pour the batter into the lined pan.
6. Microwave on High for 3 minutes and check to see if the center is still liquid or beginning to "bake."
7. Microwave 2½ to 3 minutes more, just until the batter "sets up" and seems firm (not hard) in the center. To keep these fudgelike, cook less time, adjusting the cooking time to your microwave. The brownies continue to firm as they cool, so don't rush to microwave extra minutes unless the center is *really* liquid.
8. Set the brownies in the refrigerator to chill 10 minutes before cutting them. Before serving, trim brownies around their outermost edges if they have become tough from a bit too long in the microwave.

**NOTES:**

· Two pans of this recipe will make a great Black Forest Cake (page 194). Lift the first batch out of your baking pan using the wax paper, and while this layer is chilling, microwave a second layer, and a third if a big crowd is coming!
· This recipe can be baked in a conventional oven at 325°F for 30 to 35 minutes. Omit the wax paper and spray oil the pan instead.

¼ pound (1 stick) unsalted butter

2 ounces unsweetened chocolate (premelted packets are fine)

1 cup sugar

2 eggs

½ teaspoon vanilla extract

¾ cup flour

Pinch of salt

Chopped nuts, flavored chips, marshmallows, or an icing of melted chips (optional)

**EQUIPMENT**
1-quart Pyrex cup; 8-inch square Pyrex glass pan; wax paper

coffee cakes, quick breads, muffins, brownies, blondies, and crêpes

# blondies in a pot

Cooking spray (optional)

¼ pound (1 stick) unsalted butter

1 ½ cups packed light brown sugar, or 1 cup packed dark brown sugar plus ¼ cup maple syrup

1 teaspoon vanilla extract

¼ teaspoon salt

2 eggs

1 teaspoon baking powder

2 cups flour

## EQUIPMENT
2-quart saucepan; mixing spoon; 9x13-inch baking pan

*M*elting and combining all the ingredients in a single saucepan makes for very little mess. Blondies can be dense, chewy, and a bit undercooked and no one will complain. The dark brown sugar and maple syrup make a softer and darker cake, the light brown sugar makes a denser one, and undercooking leaves them chewy.

You may want to add 1 generous cup of any mixture of the following: chopped pecans, walnuts, or cashews; coconut; dates; crystallized ginger; butterscotch chips or white, milk, or semisweet chocolate chips; Heathbar-Crunch toffee chips; raisins; chocolate-covered raisins; or Nut Brittle (page 130).

1. Preheat the oven to 350°F. Spray or butter the baking pan.
2. Partially melt the butter in the saucepan and allow it to finish melting off heat. Stir in the sugar (and maple syrup if using) and vanilla.
3. Beat in the eggs.
4. Measure the dry ingredients directly into the pot and stir just until incorporated. Add any optional ingredients you choose.
5. Pour into the baking pan and level, pushing the dough to fill the entire pan evenly. Bake 25 to 30 minutes, so the blondies are slightly undercooked but a toothpick comes out clean.
6. Let cool and cut into 3-inch bars.

i knew you were coming so i baked a **cake**

# crêpes

**Makes 12 to 15 8-inch crêpes**

*A*nxiety: *What do I do if the cake won't rise?*
*Answer: Make crêpes. They aren't supposed so.*

*The batter for crêpes isn't a magical formula. The ratios or proportions are fairly consistent from one cookbook to another. Crêpe batter is more durable than one might expect, and once the pan is actually hot enough, the crêpes cook quickly, come out of the pan easily, and are strong enough to toss around (if you have some playful helpers). Don't flip them! It isn't necessary, especially if you will heat them again to serve. Make them as thin as you like by adding extra milk or water.*

¾ cup flour

½ tablespoon sugar

2 tablespoons confectioners' sugar

¼ teaspoon baking powder

¼ teaspoon salt

1 ½ cups milk

1 egg

1 tablespoon melted butter, plus additional for the pan

**EQUIPMENT**
8-inch nonstick crêpe pan or frying pan; curved rubber spatula; 1-quart Pyrex cup or 1-quart mixing bowl and a whisk or blender or food processor; dinner plate; dish towel

1. Measure the ingredients into the Pyrex cup or mixing bowl, blender, or food processor and mix (or pulse 6 to 8 times in the blender or food processor). If you have the time, let this batter rest for 30 minutes; resting makes the crêpes lighter in texture.
2. Heat the crêpe pan on medium-high heat so the pan is hot before you grease it lightly with just ¼ teaspoon of melted butter.
3. Pour about ¼ cup of batter into the pan and swirl to coat the entire bottom, tipping the excess around the side edges to keep the crêpes thin.
4. Cook 20 seconds. Then, using the tip of the spatula, lift the edge of the crêpe and turn the pan upside down to flip the crêpe onto the plate.
5. Add a bit more butter as you repeat the pour, swirl, cook, flip routine until all the batter is used. (Stir the batter occasionally while you are making the crêpes to keep the ingredients well blended.)

**TO FILL AND SERVE:** Set one crêpe on a plate, scoop 1 heaping tablespoon to ¼ cup of filling in a column in the center. Lay one side over, onto the filling, and then flip this filled and covered part over onto the remaining third. The crêpe will now be a smooth, slightly flattened cylinder, able to be gently slid and nudged onto your serving plate, where it will be ready for a sprinkling of confectioners' sugar, or a dollop of crème fraîche or sweetened sour cream.

**QUICK TIP:** Crêpes can be made the day before, covered with a damp dish towel, and refrigerated until you are ready to fill them.

coffee cakes,
quick breads,
muffins,
brownies,
blondies, and
crêpes

**53**

*Each filling recipe makes enough to fill 12 to 15 crêpes.*

## walnut crêpe filling

2 cups ground walnuts

½ cup sugar

½ cup heavy cream

¼ teaspoon cinnamon

¼ teaspoon ground cloves

¼ cup rum

**EQUIPMENT**
2-quart saucepan; mixing spoon

1. Measure the walnuts, sugar, cream, cinnamon, and cloves in the saucepan.
2. On low heat, simmer gently about 5 to 10 minutes, stirring to blend and scraping the bottom of the saucepan to avoid scorching.
3. When the filling comes together like a lumpy paste, turn off the heat and stir in the rum, and you're ready to use it or chill it for later on. This will keep in the refrigerator or freezer for several weeks, so it's a good step to *do ahead.*
4. You will need a heaping tablespoon of filling per crêpe. You can stir in more rum for a softer texture, or if the filling becomes dry waiting in the refrigerator.

## sweetened ricotta and cherry crêpe filling

2 pounds ricotta cheese

1 tablespoon to ¼ cup honey, to taste

12 ounces canned or frozen cherries, drained and chopped

Blend together the cheese, honey, and cherries. Use about ¼ cup to fill each crêpe.

i knew you were coming so i baked a **cake**

# apple crêpe filling

To fill 12 to 15 crêpes, use 6 to 8 apples in the Sautéed Apples recipe (page 163).

# blueberry crêpe filling

Thaw and drain one 24-ounce bag of frozen blueberries, reserving the juice. Bring the juice to a boil with 1 tablespoon cornstarch and pour over the berries to coat them. Allow about ¼ cup per crêpe, or prepare Blueberry Sauce (page 177) using fresh blueberries.

# dried fruit crêpe filling

1. In a heatproof bowl, pour boiling water over the dried fruit to cover and steep for 30 minutes.
2. Drain the fruit, discarding the steeping liquid, and put the fruit in a bowl. Add the rum or liqueur to the fruit and let stand at least 30 minutes.
3. Stir in the jam or purée. Spread 1 heaping tablespoon of filling onto the center of each crêpe, top each with 1 heaping tablespoon to ¼ cup sour cream or crème fraîche.

1 ½ cups raisins, currants, dried cranberries, or dried cherries

¼ cup rum or orange liqueur

2 tablespoons apricot jam or Dried Apricot Purée (page 178)

2 to 3 cups sour cream or crème fraîche

coffee cakes, quick breads, muffins, brownies, blondies, and crêpes

# apricot purée crêpe filling

Blend the purée (page 178) with enough orange juice to reach the consistency of applesauce. Use a heaping tablespoon to fill each crêpe.

# brandied fruit crêpe filling

See the Rumtuffle recipe on page 171. Use ¼ cup per crêpe. Fold crêpe in half and spoon this juicy blend on top.

i knew you
were coming
so i baked a
cake

56

chapter three

# gilding the lily

*frostings, glazes, icings, toppings, and sauces*

## frostings and glazes

jam glazes
lemon juice glaze
orange juice glaze

## icings

buttercream
cream cheese icings
chocolate sour cream icing

## toppings

oatmeal pecan crisp topping
macaroon topping

## whipped creams

chantilly cream
chocolate whipped cream
gingered whipped cream

## sauces

butterscotch sauce I
butterscotch sauce II
butterscotch sauce III
caramel sauce i
caramel sauce ii
dulce de leche
microwave fudge sauce

**Here are a wide** range of quick toppings, frostings, and sauces that may do damage to your diet but will enhance the plainest dessert. These work on lots of desserts, and in some cases, they *are* the dessert! All can be made in fifteen minutes, and many can be stored for months, always ready to perk up a dish of fruit or a slice of plain cake.

If you're pressed for time or want to add a flourish to your presentation, try these simple but effective touches:

- Place a doily or cut-out pattern on top of a plain cake. Sprinkle confectioners' sugar through a strainer for a special finish with very little effort.
- Accent a plate with a fresh flower or leaf. Make sure your decorations aren't toxic and that they have not been sprayed with citricides if they're touching the food.
- A perfect strawberry, or one that's sliced to its shoulders and pressed down into a fan, is the perfect ornament for any fruit tart or frozen dessert.
- Cut a slice of lemon to the center. Dip it in sugar and twist it into an upright spiral. Or, use the tiniest triangular wedge of lemon or lime to accent a mousse.
- Slice a carambola (star fruit) to top some billowing cream or accent a plate of tiny treats.
- Wash a bunch of grapes and, while they are moist, dip the whole bunch in sugar. Freeze them to garnish a big plate of sweets.
- Edge a cake with a ring of chopped nuts or toasted coconut.
- Drag the tines of a fork around the sides of your frosted layer cake for a design your guests will notice.
- Don't forget **Fruit Purées** (Chapter 9), simple, bright, delicate embellishments to moisten a cake, add contrast to a fruit tart, or even top a sundae.

gilding
the lily
*frostings, glazes,
icings, toppings
& sauces*

# jam glazes

**Makes I cup**

I cup apricot, red currant,
or seedless raspberry jam

I ounce orange liqueur

½ tablespoon cornstarch
(optional)

**EQUIPMENT**
I-quart saucepan or 2-cup
Pyrex cup
Optional: pastry brush

*T*he shine of a jam glaze adds real polish and subtle flavor to a fruit tart or an open-topped pie. Try it on an Almond Torte, Baked Apples, or Cheesecake.

Melt jam on low heat in the saucepan, or microwave 1 minute on High in the Pyrex cup. Stir and repeat if necessary until the jam is melted and bubbly. Add the liqueur, stir, and spoon or brush a light layer onto your dessert. You can strain out pieces of fruit if you want to, and brush a smooth layer on top of a tart for a professional finish.

**VARIATION:**

To finish a cheesecake, cover a crack, or create a fruit topping, add 1 teaspoon cornstarch before heating the jam. Cook, stirring, until the mixture is no longer opaque. This will take 1 or 2 minutes in the microwave on High, or about 5 minutes simmering in the saucepan. The jam must come to a boil to clear and cook off the raw taste of the cornstarch. It will thicken further as it cools.

**QUICK TIP:**  Any extra glaze keeps in the refrigerator as long as jams do, ready for a 1-minute reheat and use.

i knew you
were coming
so i baked a
cake

# lemon juice glaze

**Makes about 1 cup**

*T*here is no substitute for the sparkle that fresh lemon juice and zest provide. Try this glaze on a **Butter Cake** (page 30), or glaze a Date-Nut Fruit Bread with it (page 48). It perks up Gingerbread (page 35) or an **Almond Torte** (page 40). It can also be used on plain sugar cookies.

*Juice and zest of 1 lemon (about 1 ounce juice and ½ teaspoon zest)*

*1 ¼ cups confectioners' sugar*

*Food coloring (optional)*

**EQUIPMENT**
*box grater or hand-held grater; wax paper; knife; 1-quart mixing bowl; spoon; juicer or fork*

1. Rest the grater on a piece of wax paper on the counter for easy handling and no mess. Grate the zest from the entire lemon. Tip the paper into the bowl.
2. Slice the lemon in half and juice it into the bowl.
3. Add the sugar and blend together.
4. You can add a teaspoon or two of water if this is too thick to ice your cake or cupcakes with ease. A drop of yellow food coloring will help your guests to identify the flavor before they've tasted it. (Once they've tasted it, they'll know!) Use immediately.

**QUICK TIP:**   You can keep citrus zest (lemon, orange, or lime), mixed with an equal proportion of granulated sugar, stored in an airtight container in the freezer. Squeeze the juice and keep it in another plastic container. Then, anytime you need fresh zest or juice, you're ready.

gilding
the lily
*frostings, glazes,
icings, toppings
& sauces*

# orange juice glaze

**Makes about 1 cup**

*Juice and zest of 1 lemon (about 1 ounce juice and ½ teaspoon zest)*

*¼ cup orange juice*

*1 ½ cups confectioners' sugar*

*Red and yellow food coloring (optional)*

*Additional orange or lemon juice (optional)*

**EQUIPMENT**

box grater or hand-held grater; wax paper; knife; 1-quart mixing bowl; spoon; juicer or fork

H*ere is a case where the lemon flavor isn't obvious but it enhances the orange flavor so much that it's worth the extra step. As it dries, this glaze will have some crackle to it. Adding more juice will make it thinner, easier to cut through on the cake, and more flavorful. Try topping the Orange Juice Butter Cake (page 31), the Date-Nut Fruit Bread (page 48), or the Smooth as a Baby's . . . Carrot Cake (page 39) with this glaze.*

1. Rest the grater on a piece of wax paper on the counter for easy handling and no mess. Grate the zest from the entire lemon, then tip the paper into the bowl.
2. Slice the lemon in half and juice it into the bowl.
3. Add the orange juice and sugar and blend with the spoon until the mixture is smooth.
4. Add 1 or 2 drops of food coloring if you wish and additional juice until the desired color and consistency are reached.

**NOTE:**   See Chocolate-Glazed Fruits (page 127) for an easy chocolate glaze.

i knew you were coming so i baked a **cake**

## ❧buttercream

**Makes about 3 cups, enough to fill and cover two 9-inch layers, 24 cupcakes, or the top and sides of a 9x13-inch sheet cake**

W*hy does real buttercream carry such a mystique? Here's a simple way to whip up an indulgence that holds for weeks in the refrigerator and months in the freezer. Bring it back to room temperature and whip it again, just briefly, until it reaches spreading consistency. Add your flavoring just when you're ready to use it.*

Cream the butter by beating it slowly in the mixer or by hand. Stop the mixer to add the sugar. Restart the mixer slowly, and then beat faster to incorporate to a smooth consistency. Add the cream, vanilla, and salt and continue beating until smooth. Add flavoring and whip to lighten and bring to spreading consistency, about 5 to 10 minutes on medium speed or 10 minutes using a whisk and lots of energy.

½ pound (2 sticks) unsalted butter

1 pound confectioners' sugar

½ cup heavy cream, light cream, half-and-half, sour cream, or whole milk

1 tablespoon vanilla extract

¼ teaspoon salt

Flavoring (see list)

**EQUIPMENT**
electric mixer, or 3-quart mixing bowl and mixing spoon
Optional: whisk

**VARIATIONS:**

· Add ⅔ cup cocoa powder.
· Add 1 or 2 tablespoons espresso powder or 2 tablespoons coffee liqueur.
· Add 1 tablespoon espresso powder and ¼ cup cocoa.
· Add 2 tablespoons bourbon and top the cake with pecans, Sugar and Spice Pecans (page 129), or **Praline** (page 130).
· Add juice and zest of 1 lemon.
· Add juice and zest of 1 lemon plus 2 tablespoons orange liqueur.
· Add 1 part Butterscotch Sauce (pages 72–73) to 2 parts Buttercream. Garnish with rum-soaked, strained raisins, toasted coconut, Sugar and Spice Pecans (page 129), or Praline (page 130).

**NOTE:** You may need to adjust the amounts of vanilla, salt, and even the sugar for certain flavorings, so taste the Buttercream before you're ready to use it.

**QUICK TIP:** Since this recipe easily doubles, you can make extra basic Buttercream and freeze it.

gilding the lily
*frostings, glazes, icings, toppings & sauces*

# cream cheese icings

**Makes about 3 cups, enough to fill and cover two 9-inch layers, 24 cupcakes, or the top and sides of a 9x13-inch sheet cake**

½ pound cream cheese

¼ pound (1 stick) unsalted butter

2 cups (½ pound) confectioners' sugar

1 teaspoon vanilla extract

**EQUIPMENT**
electric mixer or 3-quart mixing bowl; mixing spoon
Optional: whisk

*This icing is soft. It never becomes as firm as chilled buttercream. Be careful not to beat it long. Be sure to use regular (not low-fat or nonfat) cream cheese, and ½ cup extra sugar if you are preparing this in warm weather. This recipe doubles with no problem and holds a week or more in the refrigerator. When you're ready to frost your cake, simply remove the frosting from the refrigerator and beat for 3 minutes before using.*

1. Cream the cream cheese and butter together in the large bowl of an electric mixer until they are smooth and completely blended, about 2 minutes at medium speed with an electric mixer or 3 to 5 minutes by hand.
2. Add the sugar gradually, beating slowly at first and then increasing the speed until blended to a smooth consistency.
3. When the sugar is incorporated, increase the beating speed to lighten the icing for easier spreading, 1 or 2 minutes in an electric mixer or, if using a whisk, with more elbow grease.
4. Add the vanilla and any other flavorings you choose when the icing has reached spreading consistency.

**VARIATIONS:**   (See Buttercream (page 63) for additional suggestions.)

· Add 2 squares unsweetened chocolate, melted, plus 1 ounce orange- or coffee-flavored liqueur, or ⅔ cup cocoa powder and 1 ounce liqueur.
· Add 2 ounces maple syrup and 1 ounce rum, topped with pecans.
· Add ¼ cup Dried Apricot Purée (page 178) and the zest of 1 orange.
· Add ¼ to ½ cup orange juice and the zest of 1 orange.
· Add the zest and juice of 1 lemon.
· Serve plain, topped with toasted coconut.
· Serve plain, topped with raisins, currants, nuts, or glacéed fruits.

i knew you were coming so i baked a **cake**

# chocolate sour cream icing

**Makes about 3 cups, enough to fill and cover two 9-inch layers, 24 cupcakes, or the top and sides of a 9x13-inch sheet cake**

*T*his tangy frosting doesn't appeal to really young children, who prefer very simple sweet tastes, but it's a quick chocolate fix for a more sophisticated palate. It goes well on the **"Don't Do It" Chocolate Cake** (page 33). Add a teaspoon of vanilla if kids are coming, or try **Chocolate Whipped Cream** (page 70) instead. This icing requires regular (not low-fat or nonfat) sour cream.

*12 ounces semisweet chocolate chips*

*1 pint sour cream*

**EQUIPMENT**
electric mixer; 3-quart mixing bowl; whisk; saucepan or double boiler
Optional: 2-cup Pyrex cup

1. Melt the chocolate in the mixing bowl set over a saucepan of simmering water as a double boiler, or in the 2-cup Pyrex measure in the microwave for 15 seconds on Medium. Stir and repeat until smooth if microwaving, then pour into the mixing bowl.
2. Add the sour cream, blend, and chill at least 20 minutes.
3. Beat well for 3 to 5 minutes to lighten the texture to spreading consistency. Use immediately.

gilding
the lily
*frostings, glazes,
icings, toppings
& sauces*

# ❧oatmeal pecan crisp topping

**Makes enough to top a 9x13-inch baking pan filled two-thirds with fruit**

1 cup oatmeal

¾ cup flour

1 cup brown sugar

1 cup chopped pecans stirred with 1 to 2 teaspoons cinnamon (optional)

¼ pound (1 stick) unsalted butter, cut into ½-inch chunks or melted

**EQUIPMENT**
one-gallon zip-top bag
Optional: 1-cup Pyrex cup

*T*here's always room in my freezer for an extra bag of this topping. For an easy weeknight treat I purchase a bag of frozen sliced peaches. The peaches go into a buttered baking dish, I reach for a fistful of this topping, and a 350°F oven does the work in about 20 minutes.

1. Measure the oatmeal, flour, brown sugar, and pecans (if using) into the zip-top bag. Seal and toss around to combine.
2. Cut the butter into the bag and pinch with your fingers to blend all ingredients. Alternatively, melt the butter in a Pyrex cup in the microwave on High for 30 seconds and then blend it with the dry ingredients.
3. Store any extra in the same bag in your freezer.

**QUICK TIP:**   If you make extra of this topping it will keep well in your refrigerator for 2 weeks, or in the freezer for 2 months. Pour out just what you want to use for a crisp, to top bar cookies, or to use on a Sour Cream Coffee Cake (page 45).

**NOTE:**   See recipes for cobblers, crisps, and pies for ideas about different fruits or berries. These are great *Do-Ahead* desserts that can withstand a visit to the freezer without losing quality.

i knew you
were coming
so i baked a
**cake**

# macaroon topping

**Makes about ¾ cup, enough to spread on a 9-inch tart or an 8-inch square pan of Pâte Sucre for bar cookies, 6–8 apples or pears as topping**

*T*his recipe makes a great topping for Baked Apples or Baked Pears *(page 164). But why stop there? It also works as a layer for a Pear-Almond Pie (page 94), or on Apricot-Macaroon Bars (page 115), or as an alternative to* **Oatmeal Pecan Crisp Topping** *(page 66) for a special fruit-based dessert.*

½ can or tube (about 4 ounces) of almond paste

2 egg whites

¼ cup sliced almonds or coconut (optional)

**EQUIPMENT**
1-quart mixing bowl; fork
Optional: electric mixer

1. Soften the almond paste by pressing it with a fork against the sides of a 1-quart bowl.
2. Add the egg whites and blend them into the paste with the fork, or whip with an electric mixer to lighten the texture and make it smooth.
3. Drop by tablespoonfuls onto fruits or spread evenly onto pastry before baking.
4. Sprinkle sliced almonds or coconut on top during the last 10 minutes of baking if you like.

**NOTE:**   If you like almond flavor and appreciate the no-cholesterol and low-fat of egg whites, see the recipes for Macaroons on page 106 in the Cookies chapter.

gilding
the lily
*frostings, glazes,
icings, toppings
& sauces*

# whipped cream

Who says a little indulgence is such a bad thing? With so little effort, such billowing delight! To assuage my guilt, I used to whip cream by hand, justifying the calories burned against the fingers licked, but I'm over that now.

The softest stage of whipped cream, called "Chantilly," is barely double the volume of poured cream. It mounds a bit like a soft snowdrift or lathered shaving cream. There are no peaks; there's nothing stiff about it. Keep beating if you want to fold flavoring into the whipped cream to make something else, such as a mousse, or if you want enough body to hold up in layers, as in a fool or a trifle. But if you're just going to top a warm crisp or pie or the Chocolate Chunk Bread Pudding (page 148), let the Chantilly be the finishing grace.

Once whipped, cream begins to lose volume as it waits to be consumed. If you must whip it ahead of time, whip it to a firmer stage and hold it in the refrigerator, then dollop on top of your dessert at the last possible moment.

Cold cream, cold beaters, and a cold bowl will give you the greatest volume. Some pastry chefs set bowls into larger bowls filled with ice. This technique helps if you're trying to whip cream in the dog days of summer. Just be sure you have extra ice cubes on those hot summer days—your guests need lots of them for their drinks too. Do note that if you whip cream too long you'll wind up with fresh butter. Congratulations!

i knew you
were coming
so i baked a
cake

68

# chantilly cream

**Makes about 2 to 3 cups whipped cream**

*The softest billows of indulgence. A dollop of fresh whipped cream makes almost anything a festive dessert.*

1 cup heavy cream

2 tablespoons confectioners' sugar

1 teaspoon vanilla extract

1 ounce orange, peach, cherry, raspberry, or coffee liqueur (optional)

**EQUIPMENT**
electric mixer or 3-quart mixing bowl, chilled, and whisk

1. Pour the cream into the chilled bowl and begin whipping in an electric mixer or with a whisk, first slowly, then increasing to high speed, for about 1 minute.
2. Stop to add the sugar and begin whipping again slowly, gradually increasing the speed so the sugar won't fly out of the mixing bowl.
3. Add the vanilla and optional liqueur as soon as the sugar is incorporated, and watch for the cream to double in volume.
4. Stop whipping to check texture: You want soft billows and not much structure.

**NOTE:** I often prefer to use up some calories as I make dessert, and I find whipping cream with a whisk a very satisfying task. It takes 5 to 6 minutes. The energy expended and the speed with which you whip the cream immediately impacts the volume of the cream. It is truly gratifying to watch the direct relationship of the work formula.

gilding
the lily
*frostings, glazes,
icings, toppings
& sauces*

# chocolate whipped cream

**Makes about 3 cups, enough for two 9-inch layers, 24 cupcakes, or the top and sides of a 9x13-inch sheet cake**

¾ cup (8 ounces) semi-sweet chocolate chunks or chips

1 cup heavy cream

2 tablespoons confectioners' sugar

1 teaspoon vanilla extract

**EQUIPMENT**

1-cup Pyrex cup; electric mixer, or 3-quart mixing bowl, chilled, and whisk

*It takes about 5 minutes to make this wonderful, child-friendly cake filling. Any extra holds well in the freezer in an airtight container for a month or longer.*

1. Melt the chocolate for 15 seconds in the Pyrex cup in the microwave on Medium. Stir and repeat, 15 seconds at a time, until smooth, and then cool.
2. Pour the cream into the chilled bowl and begin whipping, first slowly, then increasing to high speed for about 1 minute.
3. Stop the machine to add the sugar and begin again slowly, gradually increasing to high speed so the sugar won't fly out of the mixing bowl.
4. Add the vanilla as soon as the sugar is incorporated and watch for the cream to double in volume.
5. Stop whipping to check texture: You want soft billows and not much structure. Drizzle in the melted chocolate and continue whipping. The volume will increase a bit more.

**VARIATIONS:**

· You can substitute 2 tablespoons cocoa powder for the chocolate, or 1 tablespoon chocolate syrup for the sugar, chocolate, and vanilla.
· For mocha whipped cream, add 1 teaspoon espresso powder to the vanilla and proceed as above.

i knew you were coming so i baked a **cake**

# gingered whipped cream

**Makes about 2 to 3 cups when whipped**

Gingered whipped cream is a special accent for peach or rhubarb desserts like cobblers, pies, or fools, and an interesting garnish for Date-Nut Fruit Bread (page 48).

3 tablespoons finely chopped crystallized ginger

1 cup heavy cream

2 tablespoons confectioners' sugar

1 teaspoon vanilla extract

**EQUIPMENT**
½-cup bowl; electric mixer, or 3-quart mixing bowl, chilled, and whisk; knife

1. Chop the ginger and put it in the ½-cup bowl. (Reserve some pieces for garnish.)
2. Pour the cream into the chilled 3-quart bowl and begin whipping in an electric mixer or with the whisk, first slowly, then increasing to high speed, for about 1 minute. Stop the machine to add the sugar and begin again slowly, gradually increasing to high speed, so the sugar won't fly out of the bowl. Add the vanilla as soon as the sugar is incorporated.
3. At the soft Chantilly stage, stop the machine and fold in the ginger by hand.

**NOTE:** If you like this flavor combination, see the recipe for Coeur à la Crème with optional ginger (page 159).

gilding the lily
frostings, glazes, icings, toppings & sauces

71

# butterscotch sauce I

**Makes about 1¼ cups**

1 cup sugar

½ cup dark brown sugar

⅓ cup light corn syrup

⅓ cup (⅔ stick) butter

½ cup heavy cream

1 teaspoon vanilla extract

½ cup ice water

**EQUIPMENT**
1-quart saucepan, ½-cup bowl, mixing spoon

*I*t isn't difficult to make the "real thing." Here's the finishing touch to a butter pecan sundae or a homemade finish to a store-bought toasted Pound Cake (see Chapter Ten). Leftovers, stored in the refrigerator in a glass jar, can be reheated in the microwave or set in a saucepan of simmering water to be used several weeks later.

1. Measure the sugars, corn syrup, butter, and cream into the saucepan and place on low heat. Stir constantly.
2. Put the ice water in a bowl next to the saucepan.
3. When the sugar mixture begins to boil, lift a bit on a spoon and allow one or two drops to fall into the ice water. At first the sugar mixture will "shatter" and break apart as it hits. As the sugars continue to cook, test one drop at a time until the mixture holds together when it hits the water. This is the "soft ball" stage. Take the mixture off the heat and stir in the vanilla. Let cool slightly before using.

# butterscotch sauce II

**Makes about ¾ cup**

¾ cup heavy cream

⅓ cup light brown sugar

2 tablespoons rum

**EQUIPMENT**
1-quart saucepan; mixing spoon

*A* somewhat simpler but no less luscious version.

1. Blend the cream and sugar in the saucepan and bring slowly to a boil.
2. Cook about 3 or 4 minutes, stirring. Check to see if the mixture is a little grainy from undissolved sugar by rubbing a drop between your fingers.
3. When the sauce feels smooth, add the rum. Serve warm.

i knew you were coming so i baked a **cake**

72

# butterscotch sauce III

**Makes about 1½ cups**

*N*o time today? Okay, here's the really *quick* way. It's fine to use as topping for Halloween cupcakes.

1 (12 ounce) bag butterscotch chips

¾ cup (6 ounces) heavy cream

**EQUIPMENT**
2-cup Pyrex cup; spoon

1. Measure the butterscotch chips and cream into the Pyrex cup.
2. Microwave 30 seconds on High, stir, and heat again, 15 seconds at a time, to melt and blend. You have a bright, opaque butterscotch sauce.

# caramel sauce I

**Makes about 1 cup**

*T*his makes a quick glaze to top cupcakes, to build a terrific sundae, to top plain baked apples or pears, or to pair with **Date Purée** (page 179) or pecans when finishing a cake. This sauce holds well in the refrigerator for weeks until you need it. Just warm it in the microwave 30 seconds and stir. Heat it again if it needs to be softer or more liquid. This version works well in the microwave.

⅔ cups heavy cream

½ cup sugar

½ teaspoon lemon juice

**EQUIPMENT**
1-cup Pyrex cup; 2-cup Pyrex cup; mixing spoon

1. Measure the cream into the 2-cup Pyrex cup and bring it just to a boil in the microwave, 2 or 3 minutes on High.
2. Heat the sugar, lemon juice, and ¼ cup water in the 1-cup Pyrex cup in the microwave for 4 to 6 minutes on High, until the mixture turns an amber color.
3. Stir the cream into the sugar syrup until smooth.

**NOTE:** To prepare this in a saucepan, simply combine the sugar, lemon juice, and ¼ cup water and simmer, stirring, until boiling produces the characteristic amber color. Then stir in the cream and serve.

gilding
the lily
*frostings, glazes, icings, toppings & sauces*

# caramel sauce II

**Makes about ¾ cup**

*2 dozen caramel candies*

*¼ cup heavy cream*

**EQUIPMENT**
2-quart saucepan; mixing
spoon

*T*his sauce works well for quick bar cookies (see Chapter Five).

Melt the caramel candy with the cream in a medium saucepan and stir until smooth.

NOTE:   This is very flexible and sticky at this point, so it's best used immediately, poured directly onto baked **Pâte Sucre** (page 111) or **Cream Cheese Cookie Dough** (page 112). Chill it for at least 30 minutes for easier cutting.

i knew you
were coming
so i baked a
**cake**

# ❧dulce de leche

**Makes about 1½ cups**

*T*his, without a doubt, makes the best caramel going. When you heat the sugars in condensed milk, they thicken and then turn amber-colored. You are halfway to Caramel and Pecan Bars (page 115), Caramel-Pecan Candies (page 123), an ice cream sundae, a pound cake or apple pie topping, or a layer cake filling. A major Building Block!

I can (14 ounces) sweetened condensed milk, whole milk, low-fat, or nonfat milk

**EQUIPMENT**
1-quart stainless saucepan set into another pan, as a double boiler; a metal or wooden (not rubber) mixing spoon

## PROCEDURE FOR STOVETOP:

1. Pour condensed milk into the top of a double boiler. Add about 1 inch of water to the lower pan and bring to a boil. Lower the heat and keep the water simmering. Set the condensed milk on top and then cover. Cook over the simmering water about 2 to 2½ hours.

2. Remove from the heat and beat vigorously. The caramel will turn caramel-colored and thicken further as it cools. Let cool before allowing anyone to touch this. Sugar this hot makes painful burns.

## OVEN METHOD:

This method is the traditional way to make custards in a water bath (bain marie). Check after 1¼ hours to see if it has reached an amber color and a pudding consistency. Bake, covered, another 15 minutes if necessary, and remember, it will continue to thicken further as it cools.

**EQUIPMENT**
8- or 9-inch pie plate; aluminum foil; roasting pan

1. Preheat the oven to 425°F.

2. Pour sweetened condensed milk into the pie plate, cover with foil, and place in the roasting pan. Add hot water to the pan, just below the pie plate rim.

3. Bake 1 to 1½ hours, or until the milk is thick and an amber color. Remove from the oven, remove the foil, and let cool. Chill before using.

## MICROWAVE METHOD:

This method, while fast, makes a drier product, more like putty than pudding. It will be a butterscotch, not amber, color, and it won't have as smooth a texture as the slow-cooking methods. This way is fine to use for Caramel-Pecan Candies or for bar cookies, carefully smoothing it onto the

gilding
the lily
*frostings, glazes,
icings, toppings
& sauces*

**75**

half-baked pastry dough. Once it has cooled, it will need to be reheated 30 seconds on High in the microwave to become pliant enough to handle. If you add one or two tablespoons of heavy cream or half-and-half when you warm it and work the cream in with a spoon, the caramel will be a bit softer.

1. Pour the condensed milk into the bowl and cover with plastic wrap. Microwave on High for 2 to 3 minutes. Remove the bowl from the microwave and open the plastic wrap *away from your face.* Stir to release the air pockets and steam and to make the caramel smooth in texture. Re-cover the bowl with fresh plastic wrap and microwave on Medium-High 2 minutes. Again, open the wrap *away from your face* and stir the caramel.
2. Repeat Step 1 once, perhaps twice more, depending on the power of your microwave. Stop when it reaches a butterscotch color and a pudding consistency. It will thicken further as it cools. Be sure to let this cool before anyone touches it.

i knew you
were coming
so i baked a
cake

76

# microwave fudge sauce

**Makes about 1½ cups**

*O*h, *that urge for fudge! That something richer, that darker-than-chocolate taste, that extra, almost bitter, warm-and-soft-on-the-tongue texture. Can you wait three minutes?*

*You can substitute sour cream, crème fraîche, heavy cream, light cream, half-and-half, or milk for the yogurt. These will result in variations in tanginess and texture, but are still good!*

2 cups (12 ounces) semi-sweet chocolate chips

2 tablespoons butter

½ to 1 teaspoon espresso powder

½ teaspoon vanilla extract

½ cup plain low-fat or vanilla yogurt (if using flavored yogurt, omit the vanilla extract)

1 ounce rum, coffee liqueur, or orange liqueur (optional)

**EQUIPMENT:**
2-cup Pyrex cup; 1-cup Pyrex cup; tablespoon

1. Melt the chocolate chips and butter in the 2-cup Pyrex in the microwave on Medium for 1 minute. Stir and repeat 30 seconds at a time, heat, and stir again until smooth (see Note).
2. Add espresso powder, vanilla, and optional flavoring. Stir to combine.
3. Add the yogurt and stir.

**NOTE:** Chocolate heated in the microwave can "seize," or grow harder when you expect it to liquefy. Seizing occurs when chocolate is heated too quickly. Use a lower power in your microwave next time. But for now, keep stirring while adding the vanilla, espresso, and yogurt. It will soften again with these additions. If it doesn't, after you've added the yogurt, warm on Low for 30 seconds and keep stirring until it recovers.

**QUICK TIP:** While warm (or gently reheated) this is a great fudge sauce for ice cream or pound cakes. It is best stored in a glass jar, which can be microwaved on Medium for 1 minute, stirred, and again held in the jar for easy use. Or you can warm the open glass jar in a saucepan of simmering water. It makes a soft cake icing, good for a Boston Cream Pie (page 32) or "Don't Do It" Chocolate Cake (page 33) or cupcakes, and while it will firm up if chilled, it never becomes a really hard icing.

gilding
the lily
*frostings, glazes, icings, toppings & sauces*

chapter four

# cobblers, crisps, and pies

*"Pies? . . . It's apple pies the menfolk like, dearie!"*
—*The Wicked Queen,* Snow White and the Seven Dwarfs

biscuits
peach and berry cobbler
personal shortcakes
fruit crisps
great fruit combinations
nick's no-roll pie crust

**fast pie fillings**
COLD FILLINGS
lemon curd
chocolate mousse
vanilla, mocha, or chocolate pudding
fruit mousse
caramel

FRUIT FILLINGS
peach
berry
apple
apricot-orange
pear-almond
pumpkin
rhubarb

Almost any baked fruit dessert with a bit of crisp, a crumbly biscuit, or a tasty crust are what my menfolk—and womenfolk—like, dearie.

# &biscuits

**Makes about 6 to 8 3-inch biscuits**

*T*hese are very adaptable biscuits indeed, forgiving of little fingers poking them, good to use for cobbling a pan of baked fruits or rolled out and cut with biscuit cutters into Personal Shortcakes (page 83), or served hot and fresh right out of the oven with butter and jam to round out a brunch. If you're going to use them as plain biscuits, double the recipe and allow two per person. They go fast!

1. Preheat the oven to 400°F.
2. Combine the flour, sugar, baking powder, and salt in the mixing bowl. Pinch the margarine into the flour mixture by hand. Add the milk and stir until the dough holds together, kneading about 15 times.
3. Pull off fistfuls for a cobbler or rustic-looking biscuits, or roll to ¾-inch thickness and cut out 6 to 8 biscuits for Personal Shortcakes. Place on ungreased cookie sheet and bake for 15 minutes.

**QUICK TIP:** To prepare this in the food processor, measure all the dry ingredients directly into the processor bowl. Pulse once or twice to mix, then cut in the margarine or shortening in ½-inch pieces. Pulse 4 or 5 times, and, with the machine on, pour the milk in through the feed tube. In 5 to 10 seconds, the dough is kneaded and ready to roll or form by hand.

**NOTE:** All biscuits and pie crusts are best eaten fresh and warm from the oven, but if you bake extra biscuits, double-wrap and freeze them. A quick reheat at 400°F. will recapture their fresh-from-the-oven quality.

3 cups flour

½ cup sugar

2 tablespoons baking powder

1 teaspoon salt

½ stick margarine or solid vegetable shortening, cut into ½-inch pieces

1 cup cold milk

**EQUIPMENT**
3-quart mixing bowl; cookie sheet
Optional: 3-inch biscuit cutters or inverted drinking glass; rolling pin

cobblers, crisps, and pies

# peach and berry cobbler

**Makes 6 to 8 servings**

*I love pairing fruits: berries with peaches, plums with pears, nectarines with cherries. Just fill your baking pan two-thirds full, leaving room for bubbling fruit juices and the cobbling top. Serve a cobbler with Gingered Whipped Cream (page 71) or your favorite ice cream or frozen yogurt.*

1 recipe Biscuits (page 81)

1 pint blueberries or blackberries, picked over and washed, or 1 (12-ounce) bag frozen berries, loosened

8 to 10 peaches, cut into ½-inch-thick slices, or 2 (12-ounce) bags frozen peach slices, broken into chunks

1 teaspoon cinnamon

¼ cup sugar or ¼ cup Cinnamon-Sugar (page 22) or ¼ cup Mixed Spices (page 22)

1 teaspoon cornstarch or 1 tablespoon tapioca

Zest of 1 lemon, ½ teaspoon nutmeg, or ¼ teaspoon ground cloves (optional)

Juice of 1 lemon

**EQUIPMENT**
9x13-inch baking pan with a 3-quart capacity

1. Preheat the oven to 400°F.
2. Place the berries and peaches in the baking pan. Sprinkle the cinnamon and any other spices you choose, the sugar, and the cornstarch around the fruit. Squeeze the lemon juice on top and toss by hand to coat the fruit.
3. Bake about 10 minutes while you prepare the biscuit batter.
4. "Cobble" the top of the peaches with ½-inch-thick fistfuls of biscuit spreading them unevenly on top of the fruit. Continue baking another 15 minutes until the biscuits are baked through and the fruit gives off bubbly juices.

**NOTE:** See pages 83 and 84 for other great fruit combinations that work under crisp or cobbler toppings.

i knew you were coming so i baked a **cake**

# personal shortcakes

**Makes 6 to 8 servings**

*I think these are best as warm biscuits with any assortment of berries, peaches, or apricots. Make them fancy with a specially shaped cookie cutter. You can prepare the parts ahead of time and assemble fruit, cream, and garnishes when you need them. Make them often; they're quick and easy, and they're never refused!*

1. Prepare biscuits, rolling the dough ¾ inch thick and cutting into 3-inch shapes. Bake for 15 minutes in a preheated 400°F oven.

2. Split the biscuits horizontally through the center, where a natural break occurs, and place the bottom halves on dessert plates. Heap on about ½ to ¾ cup fruit per serving, allowing the fruit to spill off the sides of the biscuits.

3. Set the top halves of the biscuits against the fruit at a jaunty angle. Dollop with your choice of cream toppings, and garnish if you wish.

**GREAT FRUIT COMBINATIONS:**

· For classic strawberry shortcake: 2 pints fresh strawberries, ¼ cup sugar, and ¼ cup orange juice or orange liqueur

· 2 (12-ounce) packages thawed frozen mixed berries (use the juice, sweetened with ¼ cup confectioners' sugar)

· 2 (12-ounce) packages fresh peaches or defrosted frozen peaches, with ¼ cup sugar, ½ cup orange juice, ¼ teaspoon nutmeg, and ¼ cup orange liqueur

· 2 (12-ounce) packages defrosted frozen peaches with 1 cup softened dried apricots

· 4 cups fresh, defrosted frozen, or canned blackberries (use the juice), with 1 cup fresh raspberries for contrasting garnish

---

*1 recipe Biscuits (page 81)*

*Choice of fruits (see combinations that follow)*

*2 cups Chantilly Cream (page 69), or 2 cups sour cream sweetened with ¼ cup confectioners' sugar, or 2 cups crème fraîche*

*Mint sprigs, peach slices, or perfect berries for garnish (optional)*

**EQUIPMENT**
rolling pin; 3-inch cookie cutter (round, heart-shaped, fringed-edge) or inverted drinking glass; dessert plates

cobblers,
crisps, and
pies

83

# fruit crisps

**Makes enough to top a 9x13-inch baking pan two-thirds filled with fruit, about 8 servings**

🍂 *1 recipe Oatmeal Pecan Crisp Topping (page 66)*

**filling:**

*3 pints blueberries, picked over and rinsed*

*1 tablespoon tapioca*

*1 ½ cups sugar*

*Juice and zest of 2 lemons (about 2 ounces juice and 1 teaspoon zest)*

**EQUIPMENT**
9x13-inch baking pan; 1-quart mixing bowl or a 1-gallon zip-top bag

*Good news: there's only one pan to wash. Bake this while you're having dinner. Serve warm with vanilla ice cream or tangy frozen yogurt. Double the topping recipe and freeze half for another crisp. There's always room in the freezer for a sealed bag of this. See recipes for cobblers, pies, and bar cookies for other ideas for this topping.*

1. Preheat oven to 350°F.
2. In the baking pan, combine berries with tapioca, sugar, lemon juice, and zest. Place clumps of topping on the berries. Do not press down.
3. Bake 20 to 30 minutes, until the fruit is bubbly and the topping browns.

**NOTE:**   Use ½ tablespoon tapioca and allow 15 minutes more to bake larger, chunkier fruits. You can omit the tapioca altogether if you use apples. Remember not to fill your baking pan more than ⅔ full. It's a mess when the juices run over.

**GREAT FRUIT COMBINATIONS:**

· 6 to 8 large green apples, each peeled, cored, and sliced into 16 chunks, and 1 pint blueberries, raspberries, blackberries, or cranberries. If you use fresh cranberries, add an extra ¼ cup of sugar per 1 cup of cranberries. (Reconstituted dry cranberries do not require the extra sugar. Just cover ½ cup dry cranberries with warm water for 5 minutes, drain, and use; or cover ½ cup dry cranberries with water and heat in a Pyrex cup in the microwave for 30 seconds on High, then drain and use with the apples.)

· 8 to 10 peaches and 8 to 10 plums, pitted and sliced.

· 2 pounds sliced fresh or 1 bag frozen, defrosted rhubarb and 6 to 8 plums, pitted and sliced.

· 8 to 10 peaches, pitted and sliced, with 1 pint of blueberries or raspberries, cleaned.

- 6 to 8 large green apples, peeled, cored and sliced, with Cinnamon-Sugar (page 22) substituted for granulated sugar, and ½ cup raisins or currants added.
- 8 to 10 nectarines, pitted and sliced, with 2 cups pitted fresh cherries or 12 ounces broken-up frozen cherries or a 17-ounce can drained, pitted cherries.
- 8 to 10 plums with 8 to 10 pears, pitted and sliced.

# nick malgieri's no-roll pie crust

1 ¼ cups flour

3 tablespoons sugar

⅛ teaspoon salt

¼ teaspoon baking powder

6 tablespoons (¾ stick) cold unsalted butter, cut into 8 pieces

1 large egg, beaten lightly with a fork

## EQUIPMENT
3-quart mixing bowl; fork; pie pan or tart shell
Optional: food processor

*This is easy to do by hand. However, it can also be assembled in a food processor, though the crust will be tougher and more pebble-textured. The age-old method of working the butter by hand into the dry ingredients really does make the tenderest crust.*

### TO ASSEMBLE BY HAND:
Mix the flour, sugar, salt, and baking powder in the mixing bowl. Add the butter pieces. Using your fingertips, press the butter into the dry ingredients until the mixture resembles coarse meal. Stir in the egg just to spread it through the mixture. The dough should remain dry and crumbly.

### FOR A 9-INCH PIE SHELL:
Distribute the crumbly dough over the bottom of a pie or tart pan. Using floured fingertips, press it evenly into the bottom and up the sides of the pan. Scallop the edge by pinching and slightly twisting the dough between your thumb and index finger. (Pie and tart shells can be covered with plastic wrap and refrigerated up to 2 days, or frozen up to 1 month.)

### FOR SIX 3-INCH TART SHELLS:
Divide the dough into 6 portions. Distribute 1 portion of the dough over the bottom of a 3-inch tart pan. Using floured fingertips, press it evenly into the bottom and up the sides of the pan. Use your thumb and index finger to press the dough into the ridges of the tart pan. Repeat with the remaining portions of dough and tart pans.

### TO ASSEMBLE IN A FOOD PROCESSOR:
Measure the flour, sugar, salt, and baking powder into the processor bowl. Pulse 4 times to mix. Cut the butter pieces directly into the processor bowl and pulse 10 to 15 times, until the mixture resembles coarse meal. Break the egg into the processor bowl and pulse 4 or 5 times more, then scoop the mixture into a pie shell or tart pan and pat it into place with floured fingertips.

i knew you were coming so i baked a **cake**

· For Chocolate Pie Crust: Add 2 tablespoons cocoa powder to the flour mixture, reducing the flour by 1 tablespoon.

· For Spice Crust: Add ½ teaspoon cinnamon, ¼ teaspoon cloves, and ¼ teaspoon nutmeg, or 1 teaspoon Mixed Spices (page 22) to the flour mixture.

QUICK TIP:    While you're at it, why not double the recipe and have an extra crust on hand? Press the dough into a pie or tart pan, cover tightly with plastic wrap, and freeze.

cobblers,
crisps, and
pies

# fast pie fillings

See Frozen Puff Pastry (page 195) or Cookie Crusts (page 187) for other ways to use these fillings. Single-crust pies are definitely speediest. An un-filled shell bakes in less than 20 minutes and can be used with many cold choices. Open-topped fruit pies take a bit longer to bake, but with no dough to roll and no top to tuck in and trim, you can still beat the clock.

## COLD FILLINGS

Make Nick Malgieri's No-Roll Pie Crust (page 86) and bake it, unfilled, about 15 to 20 minutes at 375°F. Any of the following cold fillings can be made ahead of time or while the crust is baking. Here are my favorites:

## lemon curd pie

Prepare **Lemon Curd** (page 156), spread it evenly in a baked, cooled pie crust, and garnish with fresh blueberries or sliced kiwis and strawberries just before serving.

## chocolate mousse pie

Make the chocolate crust variation on page 87. Mound Chocolate Mousse (page 152) generously in the shell and garnish with whipped cream and/or a drizzle of **Microwave Fudge Sauce** (page 77).

i knew you
were coming
so i baked a
cake

# vanilla, mocha, or chocolate fudge pudding pie

Make a double recipe of **Vanilla** (page 143), Mocha (page 149), or Chocolate **Fudge Pudding** (page 149) to fill a plain or chocolate crust (pages 86, 87). Whipped Cream, chopped pecans, **Microwave Fudge Sauce** (page 77), or a few cherries garnish these pies quickly. Topping a Vanilla Pudding Pie with coconut and running it under the broiler for 2 or 3 minutes makes a quick Coconut Custard Pie.

# fruit mousse pie

A Fruit Mousse (page 151) can be poured directly into a cooled crust and chilled, so the gelatin will set up right in the pie crust and the finished surface will be smooth. If you prefer to make the mousse ahead of time, scoop mounds onto the cool crust and garnish with mint sprigs, some extra pieces of fruit, or a few berries. The first has a professional look to it, the second way is merely irresistible.

# caramel pie

One recipe of **Dulce de Leche** (page 75) can become an instant pie as soon as a plain or chocolate crust comes out of the oven. Spread 1 cup of chocolate chips in an even layer on the hot crust, smoothing them with the back of a spoon as they begin to melt. Spoon on the Dulce de Leche and top with ½ cup more chips or pecans and dollops of **Whipped Cream**.

cobblers, crisps, and pies

# peach pie

**Makes enough to fill a 9-inch pie shell**

*6 to 8 peaches, pitted and sliced, or 2 (12-ounce) bags frozen sliced peaches, broken into chunks*

*½ cup light brown sugar*

*1 teaspoon nutmeg or 1 teaspoon Mixed Spices (page 22)*

*Juice and zest of 1 lemon (about 1 ounce juice and ½ teaspoon zest)*

*1 tablespoon tapioca grains or cornstarch, or 2 tablespoons flour*

*1 pint blueberries or 1 (12-ounce) bag frozen blueberries, broken up but not thawed*

*1 recipe Nick Malgieri's No-Roll Pie Crust in a 9-inch pie plate, unbaked (page 86)*

**EQUIPMENT**
2-quart mixing bowl; grater, rubber spatula; pie or tart baking pan, cookie sheet, or aluminum foil

1. Preheat the oven to 375°F.
2. Toss all the fruits and the sugar, nutmeg, lemon juice and zest, and tapioca together in the mixing bowl and place them in the unbaked shell. Press them together and down into the pie shell by hand or with a spatula. Be sure some blueberries show on top of the pie for color and contrast.
3. Bake about 45 to 50 minutes on a cookie sheet or aluminum foil (to protect the oven from drips), until you see some bubbly juices.
4. Remove and cool at least 10 minutes before serving.
5. If you want to give the pie a professional finish, top with a Jam Glaze (page 60) or serve with **Blueberry Sauce** (page 177) or **Berry Purée** (page 176).

i knew you were coming so i baked a **cake**

# berry pie

**Makes enough to fill a 9-inch pie shell**

**PROCEDURE #1:**

1. Preheat the oven to 375°F.
2. Toss the fruit, sugar, nutmeg, lemon juice and zest, and tapioca together in the mixing bowl and pour into the unbaked shell. Press the berry mixture together and down into the pie shell by hand or with a spatula.
3. Set the pie in the oven with a cookie sheet underneath to catch any drips. Bake about 45 to 50 minutes, until you see some bubbly juices.
4. Remove and let cool at least 10 minutes before serving.

**PROCEDURE #2:**

To take advantage of berries at their peak season, try this method, which does not cook all the berries.

1. Preheat the oven to 350°F, set up the pie crust, and chill it for 15 minutes. Dock it with a fork, then bake it empty, for about 20 minutes.
2. Using the same amounts of ingredients listed for Procedure #1, combine 1 cup of the fresh berries with the sugar, the nutmeg, the juice and zest of the lemon, and 1 tablespoon cornstarch, in a 1-quart saucepan.
3. Bring this mixture to a boil on top of the stove, stirring, or covered with plastic wrap in a Pyrex cup in the microwave on High for 2 or 3 minutes, repeating 30 seconds at a time if necessary.
4. When it boils, pour the mixture into the baked shell filled with the remaining (uncooked) berries. Let cool before serving.

*2 to 3 pints blueberries or 2 (12-ounce) bags frozen berries, broken apart but still frozen*

*1 cup sugar*

*½ teaspoon nutmeg, cinnamon, or Mixed Spices (page 22)*

*Juice and zest of 1 lemon (about 1 ounce juice and ½ teaspoon zest)*

*3 tablespoons tapioca grains or ¼ cup flour*

*1 recipe Nick Malgieri's No-Roll Pie Crust (page 86) in a 9-inch pie plate, unbaked*

**EQUIPMENT**
2-quart mixing bowl; grater; rubber spatula; pie or tart baking pan, cookie sheet, or aluminum foil

cobblers, crisps, and pies

# apple pie

**Makes enough to fill a 9-inch pie shell**

*6 to 8 large Granny Smith or Golden Delicious apples (about 3 pounds)*

*¼ cup sugar and 1 teaspoon cinnamon, or ¼ cup Cinnamon-Sugar (page 22)*

*Juice and zest of 1 lemon (about 1 ounce juice and ½ teaspoon zest)*

*1 recipe Nick Malgieri's No-Roll Pie Crust in a 9-inch pie plate, unbaked (page 86)*

## EQUIPMENT
9-inch pie or tart shell pan; 3-quart mixing bowl; grater; curved rubber spatula; paring knife
Optional: pastry brush

1. Preheat the oven to 375°F.
2. Peel, core, and slice the apples into the mixing bowl. Toss them with the sugar, cinnamon, and lemon juice and zest. Arrange in the pie shell and bake about 45 minutes.
3. For a professional finish, brush on some Jam Glaze (page 60) as the pie is cooling.

## QUICK TIPS:
- Mix 1 (12-ounce) bag defrosted frozen blueberries, 1 can apple pie filling, the zest and juice of 1 lemon, and put it all in a baked pie crust for an Emergency Fruit Pie.
- See Easy as Apple Pie (page 196).

# apricot-orange pie

**Makes enough to fill a 9-inch pie shell**

1. Preheat the oven to 350°F.
2. Measure the apricots into the 2-quart bowl and add the orange juice. Heat in the microwave at High for about 3 minutes.
3. Strain off the orange juice into a Pyrex cup. To the apricots in the mixing bowl add the brown sugar, currants or raisins, juice and zest of the lemon, and the optional chopped ginger.
4. Stir the cornstarch into the orange juice in the Pyrex cup until completely dissolved. Microwave on High 1 minute, then 30 seconds at a time, to bring it to a boil so the cornstarch begins to thicken.
5. Pour the hot orange juice mixture onto the fruits and mix together. Allow 5 minutes to cool, then stir in the egg.
6. Pour into the pie shell and bake about 30 minutes, until you see some bubbly juices.
7. Remove and cool at least 10 minutes before serving. You can give this pie a professional finish by brushing on Jam Glaze (page 60).

**NOTE:** If you want to use canned apricots, skip Step 2. Just strain the canned apricots and measure the orange juice and cornstarch for Step 4.

2 cups dried apricots

1 cup orange juice

½ cup light brown sugar

½ cup currants or raisins

1 ounce juice and ½ teaspoon zest of 1 lemon

2 tablespoons chopped crystallized ginger (optional)

1 tablespoon cornstarch

1 egg, slightly beaten

1 recipe Nick Malgieri's No-Roll Pie Crust in a 9-inch pie pan, unbaked (page 86)

**EQUIPMENT**
microwavable 2-quart mixing bowl; 2-cup Pyrex cup; mixing spoon
Optional: pastry brush; strainer

# pear-almond pie

**Makes enough to fill a 9-inch pie shell**

*I recipe Macaroon Topping (page 67)*

*I can (about I pound) pears, drained*

*2 tablespoons sliced almonds (optional)*

🌰 *I recipe Nick Malgieri's No-Roll Pie Crust in a 9-inch pie pan, unbaked (page 86)*

**EQUIPMENT**
9-inch tart shell; fork; I-quart bowl; strainer
Optional: pastry brush

1. Preheat the oven to 375°F.
2. Pour the Macaroon Topping evenly onto the crust. Lay the pear halves on top in a circle, narrow ends toward the middle.
3. Bake about 50 minutes until the edges of the tart are browned. Sprinkle the optional almonds on top for the last 10 minutes of baking, and brush with some Jam Glaze (page 60) as the pie is cooling.

# pumpkin pie

**Makes enough to fill a 9-inch pie shell**

1. Preheat the oven to 350°F.
2. Spoon the pumpkin purée into the mixing bowl, add the eggs, cream, sugar, salt, cinnamon, ginger, and cloves, and blend together with the spatula.
3. Pour the filling into the crust and bake about 40 minutes until top is puffed and brown. Sprinkle with the optional chopped pecans.

1-pound can pumpkin (or butternut squash) purée (not pumpkin pie filling)

2 eggs

1 cup cream

½ cup brown sugar or maple syrup

½ teaspoon salt

1 ½ teaspoon cinnamon

½ teaspoon ginger

½ teaspoon ground cloves

Or 2 teaspoons Mixed Spices (page 22) in place of the cinnamon, ginger, and cloves

½ cup chopped Sugar and Spice Pecans (page 63) (optional)

1 recipe Nick Malgieri's No-Roll Pie Crust (Spice Crust variation) in a 9-inch pie plate, unbaked (page 86)

**EQUIPMENT**
3-quart mixing bowl; rubber spatula; 9-inch pie plate or tart pan

cobblers, crisps, and pies

# rhubarb pie

**Makes enough to fill a 9-inch pie shell**

2 pounds rhubarb, trimmed and cut into 1-inch pieces, or 1 package (about 2 pounds) frozen rhubarb, slightly defrosted

1 cup sugar

2 tablespoons cornstarch

1 pint strawberries

1 teaspoon ground cardamom (optional)

Frozen yogurt or additional strawberries for garnish (optional)

🌸 1 recipe Nick Malgieri's No-Roll Pie Crust in a 9-inch pie pan, baked (page 86)

**EQUIPMENT**
1-quart Pyrex cup; plastic wrap; 9-inch pie plate or tart pan

1. Combine the rhubarb, sugar, and cornstarch in the Pyrex cup and cover with the plastic wrap. Microwave on High 5 minutes for fresh rhubarb, 2 to 3 minutes for frozen, slightly defrosted pieces.

2. Uncover *away from your face* and stir, making sure the liquid has boiled and begun to thicken. Cover with fresh plastic wrap and microwave on High 2 to 3 minutes more. Check to see that the rhubarb has a soft, pull-apart consistency and that the syrup is thickened and translucent. Stir in the strawberries and optional cardamom.

3. Pour into the baked pie shell and let cool for at least 20 minutes before serving. It's pucker-up time with frozen yogurt as a garnish. Strawberries in Orange Liqueur (page 167) is an even better topping.

NOTE: This rhubarb-strawberry combination, without the pie shell, can be dessert on its own, served with a cookie or as a topping for strawberry ice cream.

i knew you were coming so i baked a **cake**

chapter five

# cookies, bars, and small bites

## classic cookies
butter cookies, plain and fancy
scots shortbread
pecan shortbread
granny's oatmeal cookies

## egg whites only: hold the flour
meringues
beacon hill chocolate meringues
macaroons
almond jam slices

## dough-ahead treats
cream puffs
pâte sucre
cream cheese cookie dough
cookie rolls
cookie cups

## bar cookies
caramel and pecan bars
apricot macaroon bars
raspberry coconut bars
chocolate almond bars
sabrina shear's honey pecan squares
cranberry or apricot crisp bars

The big trick that all professional pastry chefs use is to make up several basic doughs well before they are needed. Then they vary these doughs by adding ground nuts, lemon zest, or cocoa powder, by cutting cookies into different shapes, or by finishing cookies with different jams, flavored chips, sugars, or sprinkles. So take a tip from the pros with this collection of cookies, which can easily be made ahead, shaped into logs, and frozen to be sliced and baked "fresh" any time you need them.

# butter cookies, plain and fancy

**Makes 6 dozen 2-inch cookies**

*T*his basic cookie dough is always waiting in my freezer. The proportions, suggested by Richard Sax, make it a first cousin to the French sable; the flavor is pure sweet butter and vanilla. It is always the first choice when I need a butter cookie to cut out Valentine's hearts, or an unadorned complement to a rich mousse. If you want to make special shapes, it does require the rolling pin and flour, but if circles are an acceptable shape for your best butter cookie, roll the dough into 10-inch logs about 2 inches in diameter, wrap well, and chill at least one hour or freeze. Slice off as many as you need to bake just when you need them.

**NOTE:** If you replace ½ cup of the flour with ½ cup cocoa powder, you'll get chocolate cookies that hold up to the optional additions.

**DO AHEAD:**
1. Cream the butter in an electric mixer or 3-quart bowl about 2 minutes. Gradually add the sugar, then the vanilla extract, and mix until smooth.
2. Beat in the eggs until fully incorporated.
3. Add ½ cup of the flour and blend slowly. Continue to add the flour slowly, mixing each addition just until blended.
4. Divide the dough into 2 batches and stir in your choice of optional ingredients. Roll into cylinders, double-wrap in plastic, and chill until firm or freeze to use at another time.

½ pound (2 sticks) unsalted butter

1 cup sugar

2 teaspoons vanilla extract

2 eggs

2½ cups flour

**optional ingredients per half batch**

- ¼ cup softened currants
- ¼ cup mini-chocolate chips
- ¼ cup finely chopped almonds, walnuts, or hazelnuts
- ¼ cup coconut
- 1 teaspoon lemon or orange zest

cookies, bars, and small bites

electric mixer or 3-quart
mixing bowl and mixing
spoon; plastic wrap; non-
stick cookie sheets, or
cookie sheets lined with
baking parchment or alu-
minum foil

**TO BAKE:**   Preheat the oven to 350°F. Slice the chilled dough into ¼-inch-thick disks and arrange on nonstick cookie sheets, or cookie sheets lined with foil or baking parchment. Bake 10 to 12 minutes.

**QUICK TIPS:**   Wrap some plain, then:

· Slice and set on cookie sheets to bake, garnished with sprinkles or glacéed cherry halves.
· Bake plain, then drizzle with some melted chocolate or Lemon Juice Glaze (page 61).
· Roll a portion of the dough ¼ inch thick on a floured surface, and, using cookie cutters dipped in flour, cut the cookies into festive shapes.

i knew you
were coming
so i baked a
cake

# scots shortbread

**Makes 25 cookies**

*T*he simplest yet richest of cookies.

1. Preheat the oven to 325°F.
2. Cream the butter in the electric mixer and add the confectioners' sugar gradually, beating and scraping down the sides for 2 minutes. Add the flour in ½-cup increments, blending just until a mealy stage is reached, *not* until it is fully incorporated.
3. With floured fingertips, pat the dough evenly into the ungreased baking pan. Prick the entire surface with the tines of a fork. Sprinkle the granulated sugar on top.
4. Bake 20 to 25 minutes, just until lightly colored at the edges.
5. Slice partway through while warm into 25 squares or diagonally for a diamond pattern, but wait until completely cooled before removing from the pan.

**NOTE:** Since butter is the major flavor in these cookies, this is the time to pull out the stops and splurge on that European brand—French, Danish—whatever your market features as a deluxe item. An American AA unsalted quality butter will always work in a pinch, however. Never make shortbread with margarine.

**QUICK TIP:** Pressed thinner, into a 9x13-inch pan, this can become the base of a bar cookie. Top with apricot jam or Nutella and chopped hazelnuts.

*½ pound (2 sticks) unsalted butter (the best quality available)*

*½ cup confectioners' sugar*

*2½ cups flour*

*1 tablespoon granulated sugar*

**EQUIPMENT**
electric mixer or 3-quart bowl and mixing spoon; 8-inch square baking pan; fork; paring knife

# pecan shortbread

**Makes about 10 dozen ¼-inch-thick disks or about 8 dozen 1-inch balls**

1 ¼ pounds (5 sticks) un-
salted butter

¾ cup sugar

½ tablespoon salt

1 tablespoon vanilla extract

3 ½ cups flour

4 cups (approximately 1 ½
pounds) chopped pecans

Confectioners' sugar (op-
tional)

**EQUIPMENT**
electric mixer or 3-quart
mixing bowl and mixing
spoon; cookie sheet lined
with baking parchment or
nonstick cookie sheets;
plastic wrap

*S*ometimes a classic is so simple and obvious that when you taste it, you know it's right. Nick Malgieri developed this cookie at the New York Restaurant School in 1980 when the students ran a restaurant and served petits-fours at the end of a meal. I personally polished off too many of them, and even came to work early to gobble one or two left from the previous day while I had my first cup of coffee. They are melt-in-your-mouth terrific. Thanks, Nick.

**DO AHEAD:**

1. In the electric mixer or large bowl, cream the butter, sugar, and salt. Add 1 tablespoon water and the vanilla and mix. Add the flour slowly, and when it is fully incorporated, mix in the pecans by hand.
2. Roll the dough into four 2x10-inch logs, wrap in plastic, and chill, or double-wrap in plastic and freeze.

**TO BAKE:**

3. Preheat the oven to 325°F.
4. Slice the cold dough into ¼-inch disks or roll 1-inch balls of dough in your palms and set them on the cookie sheets.
5. Bake for 15 to 20 minutes. To check if they are ready, you must lift one cookie off the sheet to see if the underside has a golden edge (they don't take much color on top). Sprinkle confectioners' sugar on top for an elegant finish, if you like.

i knew you
were coming
so i baked a
**cake**

# granny's oatmeal cookies

**Makes about 3 dozen 3-inch cookies**

*T*his is a recipe I brought home from a college roommate's mother, Mrs. Staubitz of Buffalo, New York. I gave it to my mother, who subsequently has made them for her grandchildren for many years, so they are known as Granny's Cookies. My son prefers my mother's rendition to mine. Make it your own with your family's favorite fruits and nuts.

1. Preheat the oven to 350°F.
2. Measure the flour, baking soda, and oats into one bowl.
3. In an electric mixer or the other bowl, cream the butter and sugar. Add the molasses, egg, vanilla, cinnamon, and salt. When the butter mixture is fully blended, add the dry ingredients, mix, and then add the dried fruits and nuts.
4. Drop by heaping tablespoons onto the cookie sheets and bake 10 to 15 minutes (they are chewier if baked the shorter time).

**QUICK TIP:**   Double this cookie recipe and bake only what you want for the occasion. You can shape the remaining dough into a 2x10-inch log, double-wrap with plastic wrap, and freeze for another time. The doubled wrap prevents the dough from tasting of the freezer, and if you bake just as you need them, the cookies always taste fresh. They go directly from the freezer to the oven as soon as you can chop or break off cookie-size pieces.

I cup flour

¾ teaspoon baking soda

I cup rolled oats

¼ pound (I stick) unsalted butter

I cup sugar

I tablespoon dark molasses

I egg

I teaspoon vanilla extract

I teaspoon cinnamon

I teaspoon salt

*For a total of I to I ½ cups, choose any of the following: ¼ cup of each, chopped: dried currants, dates, dried apricots, cherries, cranberries, figs, golden or black raisins, pears, peaches, walnuts, almonds, or pecans*

### EQUIPMENT
two 3-quart bowls; mixing spoon; cookie sheets lined with baking parchment, or nonstick cookie sheets; plastic wrap
Optional: electric mixer

cookies, bars, and small bites

Meringues (egg whites with sugar) are really simple to whip up. They can become the basis for a tremendous range of products by altering the amounts of sugar, time of whipping, baking temperatures, shaping, and/or the incorporation of different ingredients and flavorings.

When they are used for cookies, as in the following recipes, or in combinations with nuts, you really don't need to worry about "perfectly whipped" egg whites. Practice makes perfect enough.

## ✾meringues

**Makes about 2 dozen 2-inch cookies**

2 egg whites (2 ounces)

½ cup sugar

¼ cup ground almonds (optional)

**EQUIPMENT**
electric mixer; mixing spoon; cookie sheet lined with baking parchment or aluminum foil

*These soften in your mouth into a long-lasting chew, and they dissolve, leaving no fat and very few calories behind. Add ¼ cup ground almonds to this mix and enjoy the multiple tastes and textures of one simple cookie!*

1. Preheat the oven to 300°F.
2. Start whipping egg whites in an electric mixer on medium speed. When they have doubled in size, making soft snowdrifts, stop the machine, add the sugar, and continue whipping on high speed until stiff, glossy peaks form.
3. Fold in the optional ground almonds, drop by heaping tablespoons onto the lined cookie sheets, and bake about 20 minutes. They should remain light in color, dry outside but chewy inside.

**SHAPE VARIATION:** You can make larger meringues (birds' nests or dessert shell shapes) by using about ½ cup of the whipped meringue for each portion. Form a 4-inch circle, and, with the back of a spoon, build up the sides and bake 20 to 25 minutes. One egg white will yield two servings when whipped. These are ideal for fillings.

**VARIATION:** Fold 2 cups of coconut into the whipped egg whites and sugar. Press tightly together into 1-inch pom-poms with your fingers or a melon baller. Bake about 20 minutes for a golden oak color. See Coconut Confections on page 124 for a chocolate finish.

i knew you were coming so i baked a **cake**

# beacon hill chocolate meringues

**Makes about 3 dozen 2-inch cookies**

*T*hese cookies are quick, they are winners, and they hold up well for several days.

1. Preheat the oven to 350°F.
2. Melt the chocolate chips in the mixing bowl set over simmering water or in the microwave in the Pyrex cup for 30 seconds on Medium-Low. Stir and repeat until melted and smooth.
3. With the electric mixer, beat the egg whites and salt until foamy. After about 2 minutes' beating, gradually add sugar, a little at a time, and continue beating until stiff peaks form; they should stand on their own. Stir in the vinegar and vanilla by hand, and fold in the melted chocolate and nuts.
4. Drop by teaspoonfuls onto the lined cookie sheets and bake for 10 to 15 minutes. Remove from the sheets immediately.

**VARIATION:** Use ¼ cup cocoa in place of the chocolate chips. Bake 15 to 18 minutes. The cookies will be lighter in color but still chewy and delicious.

I cup (6 ounces) semisweet chocolate chips

2 egg whites

¼ teaspoon salt

½ cup sugar

½ teaspoon vinegar

½ teaspoon vanilla extract

¾ cup finely chopped nuts (walnuts, almonds, hazelnuts, pecans, or pistachios)

**EQUIPMENT**
I-cup Pyrex cup or a double boiler arrangement (1 inch of water simmering in a 2-quart saucepan, and a mixing bowl on top); electric mixer; curved rubber spatula; a teaspoon; cookie sheets lined with baking parchment or aluminum foil

cookies, bars, and small bites

# macaroons

**Makes about 2 dozen 2-inch cookies**

*7 or 8 ounces almond paste (tube or can)*

*1 cup sugar*

*2 egg whites*

**EQUIPMENT:**
electric mixer or 2-quart mixing bowl and fork; cookie sheets lined with baking parchment or aluminum foil; 2 tablespoons or a 1-inch melon baller

*T*his is the kind of cookie almond lovers keep coming back to. It couldn't be easier to assemble.

1. Preheat the oven to 300°F.
2. Soften the almond paste in the mixer, using the paddle attachment, for about 2 minutes. (If you have pliant almond paste, you can make this recipe with a fork and a mixing bowl.) The goal is to break up the almond paste and then distribute the sugar and egg whites evenly. Stop the machine, add the sugar, and blend another minute until smooth. Beat in the egg whites for 2 minutes, or until smooth.
3. Drop by tablespoonfuls or 1 inch balls onto the lined cookie sheets. These puff up as they bake.
4. Bake for 20 minutes, or until macaroons are firm to the touch, but still chewy.

**QUICK TIP:** If these or any meringues stick to the paper liner, run a wet sponge or paper towel against the underside of the liner. This will release the cookies immediately without tearing the undersides.

**VARIATION:** Top each cookie with pignolia nuts or sliced almonds before baking.

# almond jam slices

**Makes 3 to 4 dozen 2-inch cookies**

*F*or this recipe, you measure directly into the food processor, or purchase ground nuts and mix all of the ingredients together with a fork in a bowl. Line them up and bake them in batches.

1. Preheat the oven to 350°F.
2. Grind the almonds in the food processor. Add the sugar, egg whites, almond extract, and salt. Pulse to combine until the mixture pulls away from the sides of the processor, 10 to 15 pulses.
3. Using the fork and your fingers, work the dough into logs 1 inch in diameter and the length of the cookie sheet. With the top of the fork handle, flatten the logs and press a narrow channel down the middle of each one.
4. Arrange the logs on the lined cookie sheets and bake 10 minutes.
5. Spoon jam into the center channels and bake 10 to 15 minutes longer, so the jam will thicken and adhere to the logs, and so the logs themselves take on some color.
6. Allow to cool by pulling the parchment or foil off the cookie sheets, and cut on a diagonal into ½-inch slices.

**NOTE:** If you like, you can make these logs ½ inch in diameter, because they spread as they cook. You will get smaller, delicate bites, and more of them.

2 cups (9 to 10 ounces) whole almonds

½ cup sugar

2 egg whites

¼ teaspoon almond extract

¼ teaspoon salt

½ cup apricot or raspberry jam

2 tablespoons confectioners' sugar

**EQUIPMENT**
food processor; fork; cookie sheets lined with baking parchment or aluminum foil; teaspoon

cookies, bars, and small bites

# dough-ahead treats

When you have time to get a jump on things, preparing cookie bases and freezing them in batches to fit your pans makes the production much simpler. **Cream Cheese Dough** and **Pâte Sucre** are the best. If you're caught short with no dough ready to go, **Nick Malgieri's No-Roll Pie Crust** (page 86) or Scots Shortbread (page 101) will work. Even store-bought cookie rolls can be pressed into service under a homemade topping.

**QUICK TIPS:**  I like to use Pyrex baking pans. I can see if the bottom of the crust is baked through and remove the pan from the oven before the dough becomes too brown and too fragile.

If I am really rushed, I pop one of these doughs in an 8-inch Pyrex pan into the microwave for 7 to 9 minutes at Medium (check after 5 minutes), then proceed with recipes calling for partly baked crusts.

I often set this kind of open-topped treat into miniature petit-four paper cups. No one seems to mind any irregular shapes I cut, and they're easy to handle in the paper cups. The variety of colors and textures based on one dough suggests that enormous efforts were made, but all can be done with one pastry, just by changing the topping.

i knew you
were coming
so i baked a
cake

108

# ❧cream puffs

**Makes 12 to 16 4-inch puffs or finger shapes, or 24 to 30 2-inch petite puffs**

*T*his classic recipe is much simpler to prepare than you might expect, and it always makes a big impression. It's great to bake these well ahead of time, because they freeze beautifully. Then make up some **Vanilla** or Chocolate Fudge **Pudding** (pages 143, 149) lightened with whipped cream and top with Fudge or Butterscotch Sauce (pages 77, 72–73). In three steps, about ten minutes each, you've got a real crowd-pleaser.

**DO AHEAD:**

1. Preheat the oven to 400°F.
2. Bring the milk, butter, and salt to a boil in the saucepan. Turn off the heat, add the flour all at once, and, using the spatula, blend the mixture into a paste that leaves the sides of the pan.
3. With the electric mixer at slow speed, or using the whisk, vigorously beat the butter mixture to cool for about 1 minute, and add the eggs, one at a time. Keep beating until the batter is smooth, about 2 to 3 minutes. Spoon about ¼ cup of this paste for 4-inch puffs, or one heaping tablespoon for 2-inch puffs, onto one or more lined cookie sheets.
4. Bake for 20 minutes until dry, brown, and puffed. Tap one; if it sounds hollow inside, the puffs are done.

**DO AHEAD:**

1. Prepare a pudding filling and chill.
2. Prepare a sauce topping and chill.

**TO ASSEMBLE:**

1. Open each puff along a "natural fault line," or poke a hole up through the bottom, and spoon or pipe in filling.
2. Top with topping.

*1 cup milk or water*

*¼ pound (1 stick) butter*

*½ teaspoon salt*

*1 cup flour*

*4 eggs*

*One or more of the fillings listed on page 110*

*One or more of the toppings listed on page 110*

**EQUIPMENT**
hand-held electric mixer or whisk; 1-cup Pyrex cup; 2-quart saucepan, cookie sheet lined with baking parchment or aluminum foil, or nonstick cookie sheet; curved spatula; tablespoon
Optional: piping bag and tip for filling

cookies, bars, and small bites

## Fillings

Vanilla Pudding (page 143), lightened with whipped cream

Chocolate Fudge Pudding (page 149), lightened with whipped cream

Ricotta "Mousse" (page 201)

Ice cream

Flavored whipped cream

## Toppings

Microwave Fudge Sauce (page 77)

Butterscotch Sauce (page 72–73)

Chantilly Cream (page 69)

# ♣pâte sucre

**One-half batch makes a bottom crust for a 9-inch pie or a cookie base for an 8-inch pan; ⅔ to 1 batch fits into a 9x13 pan**

*T*his dough must be prepared ahead of time. It requires chilling before handling, but then is happy to be rolled into an even layer for pies or tarts, or to be pressed into shape by hand for bar cookies. It freezes beautifully, so make several batches to keep on hand.

2½ cups flour

3 tablespoons sugar

1 cup (2 sticks) cold butter, cut into ½-inch pieces

2 egg yolks

4 tablespoons ice water

**EQUIPMENT**
food processor; curved spatula; plastic wrap

### USING THE FOOD PROCESSOR:

1. Measure the flour, sugar, and butter pieces directly into the bowl of the food processor and pulse for 10 seconds. Add the egg yolks and pulse 4 times. Slowly drizzle ¼ cup ice water through the feed tube and process in short pulses until the dough just begins to hold together. If it gets mushy, you've allowed too much water, so sprinkle on extra flour as you wrap the dough.

2. Wrap the dough and chill for later use. See the recipes for bar cookies in this chapter.

### TO MIX BY HAND:

**EQUIPMENT**
3-quart bowl; paring knife; fork; plastic wrap

1. Measure the flour and sugar into the bowl. Cut cold butter into 8 pieces directly into the flour mixture. Work the butter into the flour by hand, squeezing and pinching until the mixture has a crumbly texture.

2. Add the egg yolks and blend gently by hand or with the fork to break them up and coat the bits with the flour mixture. Drizzle ¼ cup ice water, a tablespoon at a time, into the mixture and squeeze the dough together just until it begins to form a ball.

3. Wrap and chill for later use.

**NOTE:** Collect the egg whites and freeze them in plastic containers, labeling the number of whites (which equals the number of ounces they make), to use in Egg Whites Only Cookies (page 104–7), **Almond Torte** (page 40), muffins, Smooth as a Baby's . . . Carrot Cake (page 39), Anita Farber's Banana Cake (page 34), and Date-Nut Fruit Bread (page 48).

# ❦cream cheese cookie dough

**One batch makes 4 rolls (15 to 20 cookies each); ¼ batch makes approximately 18 1½-inch cookie cups; ½ batch fills a 9x13 or 8-inch square pan for bar cookies**

½ pound cream cheese, softened

½ pound (2 sticks) unsalted butter, softened

2 cups flour

¼ cup cream, an extra ½ cup flour, and 1 teaspoon salt for more savory fillings; or 2 tablespoons confectioners' sugar and ½ teaspoon vanilla extract for a sweeter dough (all optional)

**EQUIPMENT**
electric mixer or food processor or 2-quart mixing bowl and mixing spoon; plastic wrap

*T*he basic proportions for these cookies are found in many cookbooks. Some people like the richness of added cream. Some like the sweetness of sugar in the dough. Some like it plain, just to carry the filling flavors. I do not find major differences in handling them or in the final products.

It's the shaping, minimal *handling*, and tasty fillings that make the differences. Most important is the minimal handling. Work quickly on a flour-strewn surface so the dough won't melt or stick. Marble or granite surfaces are preferred by pastry chefs for all pastry work, but a Formica counter is fine, as long as it is not located too close to a heat source.

Chill the dough so you can use it hours later, or the next day. Freezing is fine, although setting up your cookie rolls or cookie cups and then freezing them makes more sense to me.

Bake them fresh when you need them. This is a sturdy dough, and tears are easily repaired by pinching in extra pieces, but the handling involved will often result in shrinkage—the dough will pull away from the pan sides. Toppings that adhere to the surface of the dough and aren't too runny are the best choices.

Blend the cream cheese and butter and add the flour just until incorporated. Wrap and chill before proceeding.

i knew you
were coming
so i baked a
**cake**

# cookie rolls

1. On a cool, well-floured surface, divide the dough into four parts. Roll one piece out into a ¼-inch-thick rectangle roughly 8x14 inches.
2. Cover the entire surface with your choice of filling.
3. Dip your spatula in flour and run it underneath the dough to be sure it isn't stuck anywhere. Then, using your spatula to lift the long edge, roll this rectangle up tightly along its length, ending with the opening tucked underneath.
4. Wrap in plastic, or cut the log in half for easier fit in the freezer. Refrigerate or freeze at this point. When the roll is cold and firm, slice across the log into ¼- to ½-inch disks, making 15 to 20 pieces, and bake at 350°F for about 15 to 20 minutes (longer if you cut them thicker).

**EQUIPMENT**
rolling pin; 8-inch spatula; cookie sheets lined with baking parchment or aluminum foil, or nonstick cookie sheets, or 8-inch square or 9x13-inch baking pan; 8-inch offset spatula; plastic wrap

## Fillings
Use about ¼ cup of any of these per roll:

- Raisins, nuts, Cinnamon-Sugar (page 22)
- Dried Apricot Purée (page 178), Prune Purée (page 179), or Date Purée (page 179)
- Chopped nuts and Cinnamon-Sugar
- Currants and sugar
- Raspberry or apricot jam, with or without nuts
- Jam and chocolate bits
- Nutella

cookies, bars, and small bites

# cookie cups

**EQUIPMENT**
2 mini-muffin pans

*I*f you have a lot of "kid helpers" eager for a kitchen project, hand each a mini-muffin tin with openings about 1½ inches in diameter and not more than 1 inch deep. Divide one-fourth of the cream cheese dough into eighteen ½-inch cubes and show your helpers how to push the dough into the cup with a thumb, spreading it along the bottom and up the sides just over the top. These minicups can be baked in a 350°F oven for 10 to 12 minutes, cooled, and filled with an assortment of delicious and colorful fillings. Your little helpers will take a major step in their baking careers while they're finishing desserts for you.

**FILLINGS:**

- Mix ½ cup peanut butter with 1 tablespoon brown sugar. Place 1 tablespoon in each minicup and top with chocolate chips.

- Melt 3 or 4 chocolate chips in the cups while they're hot from the oven. Spread the chips around to line the cups with chocolate and fill each with a teaspoon of raspberry, strawberry, or apricot jam.

- Mix ½ cup ricotta cheese with 1 tablespoon honey or 2 tablespoons confectioners' sugar. Place 1 teaspoon in each minicup. Top with ¼ teaspoon jam or some softened currants, raisins, or glacéed fruits.

- Mix ½ cup softened cream cheese with 1 tablespoon sour cream or heavy cream and 1 tablespoon confectioners' sugar. Use 1 teaspoon per cup topped with a slice or dice of strawberry, peach, cherry, or berries (fresh, canned, or frozen, defrosted, drained). If you use frozen fruit, pat dry on paper towels.

- Whip ½ cup heavy cream with 1 tablespoon confectioners' sugar, then fold in ½ cup cranberry sauce. Use 1 teaspoon per cup, topped with ¼ teaspoon cranberry sauce or a bit of orange zest.

- Chocolate Fudge Pudding, 1 teaspoon per cup.

- Vanilla pudding garnished with chopped pecans, coconut, or butterscotch chips.

- One teaspoon Fruit Purée (pages 165, and 176–79) blended with ¼ cup sour cream, ½ cup whipped cream, or ½ cup cream cheese in each cup, garnished with coconut, a chocolate chip, or chopped nuts.

- Put 3 or 4 chocolate chips in each cup and warm again for 1 or 2 minutes in the muffin pan to melt the chips. Spread the chocolate with a teaspoon to coat the inside of the cup. Let them cool and then scoop on a bit of sorbet or ice cream, using a small melon ball scoop.

## caramel and pecan bars

**Makes about 2 dozen 2-inch square pieces**

1. Preheat the oven to 350°F.
2. Using your fingertips, press the dough evenly in a ¼-inch layer in the bottom and about ½ inch up the sides of the pan.
3. Bake for 20 minutes. Spread the caramel evenly over the dough. Press the nuts or coconut into the caramel and sprinkle the optional chocolate chips on top. Bake 2 to 5 minutes longer to melt the chocolate. Draw your knife through the chocolate to spread it over the top, then chill the pan for 10 minutes.
4. Cut into 2-inch squares.

½ batch Pâte Sucre or Cream Cheese Cookie Dough (pages 111, 112)

1 recipe Caramel Sauce or Dulce de Leche (pages 73, 74, 75)

½ cup chopped pecans or ¼ cup toasted coconut

1¼ cups chocolate chips (optional)

**EQUIPMENT**
1-quart saucepan or 1-quart Pyrex cup; 8-inch square Pyrex baking pan; 8-inch offset spatula; sharp knife

## apricot macaroon bars

**Makes about 2 dozen 2-inch square pieces**

1. Preheat the oven to 350°F.
2. Using your fingertips, press the dough evenly in a ¼-inch layer in the bottom of the baking pan and bake 10 minutes to set.
3. While the pastry is baking, mix the sugar and egg whites into the almond paste with the fork.
4. Remove the partially baked pastry from the oven and spread the apricot purée evenly on the warm pastry. Spread the macaroon mixture unevenly on top in ½-teaspoon lumps and bake about 10 to 15 minutes longer, until some golden color touches the peaks of the macaroon mixture.
5. Mark 1½-inch squares on the pastry while still warm, but allow to cool completely before you cut all the way through.

½ recipe Pâte Sucre (page 111) or Cream Cheese Cookie Dough (page 112)

½ cup sugar

2 egg whites

4 ounces almond paste

1 cup Dried Apricot Purée (page 178) or apricot jam

1 recipe Macaroon Topping (page 67), omitting the sugar and finishing with sliced almonds or coconut

**EQUIPMENT**
8-inch square baking pan; 8-inch offset spatula; 1-quart bowl; fork; paring knife

cookies, bars, and small bites

# raspberry coconut bars

**Makes about 2 dozen 2-inch square pieces**

½ batch *Pâte Sucre* or *Cream Cheese Cookie Dough (pages 111, 112)*

*1 cup raspberry or apricot jam*

*2 cups (7 ounces) coconut*

**EQUIPMENT**
8-inch square pan; 8-inch offset spatula or tablespoon; paring knife

1. Preheat the oven to 350°F.
2. Using your fingertips, press the dough evenly in a ¼-inch layer in the bottom of the pan and bake 15 minutes, or until it takes on color and is almost done.
3. Spread the jam evenly on the pastry using the spatula or the back of the spoon. Sprinkle coconut on top, and bake another 8 to 10 minutes.
4. Mark 1½-inch squares on the pastry while still warm, but allow to cool *completely*, at room temperature or in the refrigerator, before you cut all the way through.

**NOTE:**  If you want more color on the coconut, heat the broiler while you are marking off the squares. Then place the pan directly under the broiler for 30 seconds—you must watch carefully because coconut burns very quickly.

**VARIATION:**  Drizzle Microwave Fudge or Caramel Sauce (pages 77, 73) in a crisscross pattern on top of the jam layer.

# chocolate almond bars

**Makes about 2 dozen 2-inch square pieces**

1. Preheat the oven to 350°F.
2. Using your fingertips, press the dough in an even ¼-inch layer in the pan. Bake for 20 minutes, until lightly colored at the edges; the dough should be dry throughout.
3. Spread chocolate chips onto the warm crust and bake for 2 minutes more, just to melt the chocolate. With the spatula or the tablespoon, spread the chocolate evenly on the dough. Top with chopped nuts and press them into the melted chocolate.
4. Refrigerate for 10 minutes or more to set the nuts into the chocolate, then cut into 1x2-inch rectangles.

**VARIATIONS:**

· Top the chocolate with coconut.
· Use a mixture of white and dark chips. When they have melted, swirl them together with a knife to create a marble effect. Mix in the almonds.
· Use peanut butter chips topped with chopped peanuts.
· Try butterscotch chips topped with Praline (page 130).

*½ batch Pâte Sucre or Cream Cheese Cookie Dough (pages 111, 112)*

*I cup semisweet, milk chocolate, or white chocolate chips, or a mixture of all three*

*¾ cup chopped or sliced almonds*

**EQUIPMENT**
8-inch square baking pan; 8-inch offset spatula or tablespoon; paring knife

cookies, bars, and small bites

# sabrina shear's honey pecan squares

**Makes fifty to sixty 1-inch pieces**

⅔ to 1 recipe Pâte Su-
cre (page 111)

½ pound (2 sticks) unsalted
butter

½ cup honey

¼ cup granulated sugar

1 cup dark brown sugar

¼ cup heavy cream

1 pound whole pecans or
broken pieces of pecan
(about 2½ cups)

**EQUIPMENT**
9x13-inch baking pan; 2-
quart saucepan; wooden
mixing spoon

*H*ere's my favorite idea of what to do with a batch of **Pâte Sucre.**
*These are rich, and the honey keeps them chewy. They also freeze well, so
they can be made well ahead.*

1. Preheat the oven to 350°F.
2. Using your fingertips, press the chilled dough in a flat ¼-inch layer in
   the bottom of the baking pan. Bake about 15 minutes.
3. In the saucepan, melt the butter with the honey, granulated sugar, and
   brown sugar over medium heat. Do not stir; just watch as it comes to a
   boil, lower the heat, and simmer for 2 minutes. Remove the pan from
   the heat and add the cream. Stir to blend, then add the pecans and stir
   to coat them all.
4. Remove the dough from the oven. Check to make sure that the surface
   is dry and mostly cooked through. Pour the pecans and sauce onto the
   dough, spreading evenly across the surface, and bake another 20 to 25
   minutes until you see bubbles on the surface.
5. Allow to cool in the pan before cutting into 1-inch bites or 2-inch
   squares.

**QUICK TIP:**  In a pinch, you can use **Nick Malgieri's No-Roll Pie
Crust** (page 86) as a base. Double the Pie Crust recipe to be sure you
have enough for a 9x13-inch pan.

i knew you
were coming
so i baked a
**cake**

# cranberry or apricot crisp bars

**Makes about 12 small pieces, or 8 warm dessert servings**

*L*eftover cranberry sauce? Nobody will mind it served this way the next day, or the next week.

**DO AHEAD:**

1. Prepare the topping.

**TO FINISH:**

2. Preheat the oven to 375°F.
3. Use half the Crisp Topping pressed into the pan as cookie base and half as the topping, or use ½ batch **Pâte Sucre** as base.
4. Spread cranberry sauce or apricot purée evenly onto the base.
5. Use ½ Crisp recipe as topping.
6. Bake 40 to 45 minutes, until brown. These bars are crumbly to cut when warm, but topped with some crème fraîche, yogurt, or ice cream, no one minds. When chilled, they cut easily into 2x3-inch bars. They can be kept in a sealed cookie tin for several days.

1 cup whole-berry cranberry sauce, or 1 cup Dried Apricot Purée (page 178) or apricot jam

½ to 1 recipe Oatmeal Pecan Crisp Topping (page 66) or ½ batch Pâte Sucre (page 111)

*Crème fraîche, frozen yogurt, or ice cream (optional)*

**EQUIPMENT**
8-inch square baking pan; 4-inch spatula or tablespoon; paring knife

cookies, bars, and small bites

chapter six

# candies and confections

caramel-pecan candies
coconut confections
peanut butter truffles
dried fruit truffles
chocolate-glazed fruit
honeyed walnuts
sugar and spice pecans
nut brittle or praline
water cracker almond bark

Here's the chapter for those times you must impress the empress express and don't want your kitchen left a mess. A variety of little bites tease people's palates into believing that you went to great lengths.

Several of these preparations can be done days or weeks ahead of time, so I prepare two or three whenever I can and then mix a few on a plate, perhaps with cookies sliced from a roll in the freezer.

Most people are willing to start with little bites of decadence and then come back for more as a preferred dessert—they'll skip the potatoes, thank you, but please pass the truffles, again.

# caramel-pecan candies

**Makes 1 dozen generous candies**

*T*hese candies are really rich and impressive. When set into petit-four paper cups, they look as if you spent hours in the kitchen, but you can boil water, melt chocolate gently, and use a teaspoon, right?

6 ounces fine quality semi-sweet, milk, or white chocolate or a mixture, finely chopped or in chips

1 ounce heavy cream or butter

2 ounces  Dulce de Leche (page 75)

2 ounces pecans or other nuts of your choice

**EQUIPMENT**
½ cup Pyrex bowls (one per kind of chocolate) or 2-quart saucepan and 1-quart mixing bowls (one per kind of chocolate); cookie sheet lined with baking parchment or aluminum; teaspoon
Optional: petit-four paper cups

1. Gently melt your chocolate and cream or butter in the Pyrex bowls in the microwave on Low for 30 seconds. Stir and repeat, heating 15 seconds at a time until the chocolate is melted and stirred smooth. Alternatively, set up a double boiler of water simmering in the saucepan with the chocolate in a mixing bowl on top, so it heats gently.
2. Make pools of melted chocolate (about 1 teaspoon each) on the lined cookie sheets, forming circles with the back of a spoon. Allow the chocolate to cool and harden (a quick chill in the refrigerator will set them up in 2 minutes). Reserve remaining melted chocolate mixture and keep warm.
3. Place ½ teaspoon Dulce de Leche on each chocolate circle. Press nuts, broken or whole, into the Dulce de Leche. Spoon drizzles of chocolate on top to cover and encase the Dulce de Leche. Here is where a mixture of chocolates has the greatest effect. Set a whole nut on top of each candy as a garnish.
4. Chill to firm, and serve in petit four paper cups for a nice presentation.

**VARIATION:** Mixed chocolate combinations are the most fun. Use a separate glass or Pyrex bowl (and a bit more cream or butter) for each type if you choose to use a variety.

**QUICK TIP:** You can chill these at any step along the way if necessary.

candies and confections

# coconut confections

**Makes 12 to 16 confections**

¼ cup condensed milk (full, low-, or nonfat)

½ teaspoon vanilla extract

Pinch of salt

1½ cups (about 5 ounces) shredded coconut

¼ cup currants or raisins or ½ cup additional tiny chocolate chips (optional)

½ cup semisweet chocolate chips

**EQUIPMENT**
1-quart mixing bowl; fork; 1-cup Pyrex cup; cookie sheet lined with baking parchment or aluminum foil

*You really don't want to whip egg whites? But you really love Mounds Bars? Okay, try this.*

1. Preheat the oven to 350°F.
2. Measure the condensed milk, vanilla, salt, coconut, and any optional ingredients into the mixing bowl, and blend together with a fork. Form into 1- to 1½-inch balls, *pressed tightly together* with the fork and your fingers. Set on the lined baking sheet.
3. Bake about 12 to 15 minutes, until the color reaches an irresistible oak tone. Let the candies cool on the baking parchment (remove the paper to your counter or onto a plate).
4. Measure the ½ cup chocolate chips into the Pyrex cup and warm in the oven (turned off), or microwave about 30 seconds on Medium. Repeat heating if necessary, 15 seconds at a time, just to melt the chocolate.
5. Dip the tops of the balls in the chocolate, holding them skewered with the fork inserted in their bottom (flat) side, and then set them upright again on the baking parchment to cool completely. Two minutes of chilling in the refrigerator speeds up the process.

# peanut butter truffles

**Makes about 2 dozen ¾-inch balls**

*H*ere's a no-sweat sweet for those who need a peanut butter fix.

1. Bring the peanut butter and cream cheese to room temperature by setting out for 20 minutes or by microwaving at Medium for 20 seconds.
2. Stir in ¼ cup confectioners' sugar and blend smooth. Stir in the chips.
3. Form teaspoonfuls of the mixture into ¾-inch balls between your palms and roll in the optional ¼ cup of confectioners' sugar, or melt 2 ounces of chocolate in the Pyrex bowl and roll the peanut butter truffles partially in the chocolate. Chill.
4. Serve as one choice among your cookies and fruit, presented in the optional petit-four cups.

*½ cup peanut butter, smooth or chunky*

*2 tablespoon cream cheese*

*¼ cup confectioners' sugar*

*½ cup mini chocolate chips*

*Additional ¼ cup confectioners' sugar, or 2 ounces semisweet or milk chocolate (optional)*

**EQUIPMENT**

*I-cup Pyrex cup; teaspoon; ½-cup Pyrex bowl
Optional: petit-four paper cups*

candies
and
confections

# dried fruit "truffles"

**About sixty 1-inch truffles**

¼ pound pitted dates

½ pound figs

½ pound apricots

¼ pound raisins

1 cup walnuts

1 teaspoon orange zest
(from 1 orange)

¼ cup orange juice

2 or 3 ounces black currant
or orange liqueur

Coconut or extra chopped
nuts as a coating (optional)

## EQUIPMENT
food processor; curved
spatula; 8-inch square baking pan or 9x4-inch loaf
pan; plastic wrap; petit-four
paper cups

*C*hocolate truffles always present a problem in the dog days of summer, either melting or sweating before they are consumed. Here is an alternative nonchocolate candy that can be made well ahead, keeps in the
refrigerator for weeks, and won't melt in the summer.

**DO AHEAD:**

1. Everything except the optional coating nuts goes into the food processor. Pulse until the pieces are no larger than ¼ inch.
2. Press the mixture flat into the pan and cover the surface with plastic
   wrap. Chill at least 1 hour for easier handling—longer allows the flavor
   of liqueur to mellow.
3. Scoop out a teaspoonful at a time, pinch and roll with your fingers into
   a ball, and place in petit-four paper cups to serve, or roll the balls in coconut or chopped nuts and then set them in the petit-four cups.

**NOTE:** Add more liqueur, 1 ounce at a time, if you want to preserve this
mixture for several weeks. You can alter the proportions of the fruits without harm, and they are colorful and delicious any season.

i knew you
were coming
so i baked a
cake

# chocolate-glazed fruit

**Depending on the size of the fruits and the thickness of the chocolate coating, covers 3 to 4 pints of strawberries**

*T*hese luscious morsels make an elegant end to a dinner party and are very easy to make. I have a small frying pan with straight sides, which I set on top of a matching 2-quart saucepan. I like the low sides of this frying pan because I can dip strawberries, dried fruits such as pears or peaches cut in half, or small pieces of crystallized ginger without having to use enormous quantities of chocolate, or having to reach deep into a hot pot. Hold any leftover chocolate in a plastic container in the refrigerator to reheat gently another time to use as a chocolate glaze.

*1 pound semisweet chocolate, milk chocolate, or white chocolate, cut into ½-inch chunks, or chocolate chips*

*2 tablespoons canola oil*

*Strawberries, dried fruits, or crystallized ginger*

**EQUIPMENT**
double-boiler setup or 1-quart mixing bowl set onto a 2-quart saucepan with 1 inch of simmering water, cookie sheet lined with baking parchment, aluminum foil, or wax paper

**TO MAKE THE GLAZE:**

1. Bring 1 inch of water to warm in the lower part of the double boiler, or set a saucepan of water under the mixing bowl on low heat. Add the chocolate and oil to the top pan or mixing bowl and stir as it melts. The glaze is ready when the chocolate mixture is completely melted and smooth.

**TO DIP THE FRUIT:**

2. Lower the heat under the simmering water and begin to dip your fruits, starting with the largest pieces. Dip strawberries halfway to two-thirds into the chocolate, allowing the bright red color to peep out above the shoulders. Carefully wipe one side of the berry against the side of the pot and place this side down on your cookie sheet. As the chocolate cools it will pool, so try to avoid a heavy "foot" collecting where the berry stands. Follow the same procedure for dried fruits or crystallized ginger.

**NOTE:** This does not work well with cut fresh fruits because the juice repels the chocolate. Strawberries, if very fresh and not bruised, work well but *must* be eaten that day or they weep and discolor the chocolate. Dried fruits and glacéed fruits, with their heavy sugared surface, hold up for several days, as does crystallized ginger.

candies
and
confections

# honeyed walnuts

**Makes ½ cup**

½ cup walnuts or pecans

2 or 3 tablespoons honey

**EQUIPMENT**
cookie sheet lined with
aluminum foil; tablespoon

*I* usually make larger batches of these nuts. They seem to get nibbled whenever they are available, and extras become a garnish for sundaes or toasted pound cake, or a crunchy finish to fruit compotes.

1. Preheat the oven to 400°F.
2. Put the nuts on the lined cookie sheet. Spread honey on them, tossing with the spoon or your fingers to coat unevenly. (If they are completely coated, they will be too sweet.)
3. Roast about 5 to 8 minutes. When the honey bubbles and the nuts give off fragrance, they are done.

**NOTE:** For this small quantity, the tray in a toaster oven can be lined with foil and will toast these nuts very well. When I expect a crowd of 10 to 15 guests, I use 10 ounces (2½ cups) walnuts and approximately ½ cup honey and put them on a large cookie sheet.

i knew you
were coming
so i baked a
cake

# sugar-and-spice pecans

**Makes 1 cup coated nuts**

*T*hese are great to prepare as guests arrive—their fragrance perfumes the house and offers a warm welcome. If there are leftovers, they can top ice cream, be chopped to top a cake, or be ground quite fine to flavor buttercream.

1. Preheat the oven to 400°F.
2. Place the egg white in one of the bowls and toss the nuts around in the egg white to coat.
3. Put the spices in the other bowl and toss the nuts to coat.
4. Spoon the coated nuts onto the lined cookie sheet. Roast 5 to 10 minutes to dry the egg white completely, tossing to separate the pecans while they are roasting.

**QUICK TIP:**  I keep a jar of Mixed Spices (page 22) on hand in my pantry and find many uses for them.

1 egg white

1 cup pecans

½ cup Mixed Spices (page 22)

**EQUIPMENT**
cookie sheet lined with aluminum foil; two 1-quart mixing bowls; teaspoon

candies
and
confections

# nut brittle or praline

**Makes 3 cups broken brittle or 2 cups ground praline**

1 ½ teaspoons butter

½ cup light corn syrup

1 cup sugar

1 cup pecans, peanuts, cashews, or almonds, whole or slightly broken

1 ½ teaspoons vanilla extract

1 teaspoon baking soda

**EQUIPMENT**
1-quart Pyrex cup; mixing spoon; cookie sheet lined with aluminum foil; food processor (for Praline)

*T*his is a remarkably simple way to make a candy, and when crushed in the food processor, this Praline adds a wonderful burnt-sugar crunch to a variety of desserts.

Praline keeps almost forever in a plastic container in the refrigerator. Use it to top ice cream sundaes, baked apples, or fruit compotes. Stir it into Buttercream (page 63) as a flavoring, or sprinkle it on top of an iced cake for crunchy contrast. It can top a bar cookie, blend into a cookie dough, finish off Caramel-Pecan Candies (page 123), or accent a triple crème dessert cheese such as St. André.

Baking soda makes this candy easier to chew without cracking your teeth, but if you prefer the candy to remain clear and just want to make Praline, you can leave it out with no harm to the recipe.

1. Grease the lined cookie sheet with ½ teaspoon of the butter.
2. Combine the corn syrup and sugar in the Pyrex cup. Microwave on High for 4 minutes. The corn syrup will boil but remain clear and white.
3. Stir and then add the nuts. Microwave on High for 5 minutes until light-brown and fragrant.
4. Stir in the remaining 1 teaspoon of butter and the vanilla, blend well, and microwave on High 1 to 1½ minutes more for a rich amber color.
5. Add the baking soda and stir gently. This will foam and grow right to the top of the cup! Pour onto the prepared baking sheet. Let cool and break into serving pieces or grind into praline with a few pulses in the food processor.

**NOTE:** Melted sugar can be dangerously hot, but if you use the microwave, there's much less risk of burning yourself.

i knew you were coming so i baked a **cake**

# water cracker almond bark

**Makes about 2 pounds**

*T*his one is outrageous! It might change you into a candymaker, and it makes a different treat for Passover.

1. Preheat the oven to 375°F.
2. Build up a ½-inch edge of foil all around the cookie sheet. Spread 1 teaspoon of butter on the lined sheet. Cover the surface of the pan with coarsely broken crackers or matzo. Sprinkle almonds or pecans on top.
3. Melt the rest of the butter in the saucepan. Add the brown sugar and boil gently over medium heat until thick and syrupy, about 5 minutes.
4. Drizzle this mixture evenly over the crackers and nuts and bake for 8 to 10 minutes. It will not seem like enough coverage, but as it bakes, it spreads.
5. Remove from the oven and sprinkle on the chips immediately. Allow the chips to melt for about 5 minutes before spreading them with the back of a spoon.
6. Let cool and break into pieces to serve. This stores well in an airtight container in the refrigerator for one week.

½ pound (2 sticks) unsalted butter

1 box (4 ounces) plain water crackers or 4 sheets plain matzo

1 cup (4 to 5 ounces) whole roasted almonds or pecans

1 cup dark brown sugar

1 (12-ounce) package milk chocolate chips or semisweet chocolate chips

**EQUIPMENT**
cookie sheet lined with aluminum foil; 2-quart saucepan; mixing spoon

So I Baked a Cake · So I Baked a Cake · So I Baked a Cake · So I Baked a Cake · So I Baked a Cake · So I Baked a Cake · So I Baked a Cake

chapter seven

# frozen desserts

amy cotler's earl grey granita
amy cotler's orange-chocolate granita
mango sorbet
semifreddo (frozen chocolate mousse I)
frozen bananas

These, of course, must be prepared ahead. They are great summer desserts but really work year-round. Accent them with plain cookies, a chocolate mint stick candy, or some fresh fruit.

# amy cotler's earl grey granita

**Makes 4 servings**

*Y*ou can make a cup of tea, right? Then you can make granitas, which are basically Italian ices. Garnish with a strawberry sliced to the shoulder and fanned, and pass around biscotti or Butter Cookies (page 99).

¼ cup honey

¼ cup sugar

3 Earl Grey tea bags

2 tablespoons (1 ounce) lemon juice

Sliced strawberries as garnish (optional)

**EQUIPMENT**
2-quart saucepan; mixing spoon; two ice-cube trays or a plastic storage container; food processor or blender

**DO AHEAD:**

1. Bring 2¼ cups water, the honey, and the sugar to boil in the saucepan and boil for 1 minute, stirring to dissolve the sugar. Lower the heat to a simmer, drop in the tea bags, cover, and steep for 10 minutes; turn off the heat.

2. Remove the tea bags and stir in the lemon juice. Pour the mixture into the ice-cube trays and freeze until solid.

**TO FINISH:**

3. When you are ready to serve, empty one ice-cube tray into the food processor or blender. Pulse about 10 times or until there are no large chunks and the mixture is granular but not puréed. Remove to chilled serving bowls and hold in the freezer while you repeat the processing with remaining frozen tea mixture. Serve immediately, garnished with sliced strawberries if you like.

frozen
desserts

135

# amy cotler's orange-chocolate granita

**Makes 4 servings**

¼ cup cocoa

½ cup sugar

1 ½ cups orange juice

1 tablespoon orange liqueur

*Fresh orange segments or well-drained canned mandarin oranges, and mint sprigs, for garnish (optional)*

## EQUIPMENT

2-quart saucepan; rubber spatula; two ice-cube trays or a plastic storage container; food processor or blender

*G*arnish each portion of this granita with some orange segments and a chocolate mint stick candy.

### DO AHEAD:

1. Bring ½ cup water, the cocoa, and sugar to a boil in the saucepan. Boil for 1 minute, stirring to combine the ingredients and dissolve the sugar. Remove from the heat and stir in the orange juice and orange liqueur.
2. Pour the mixture into the ice-cube trays and freeze until solid.

### TO FINISH:

3. When you are ready to serve, empty one ice cube tray into the food processor or blender. Pulse about 10 times or until there are no large chunks and the mixture is granular, but not puréed.
4. Remove to chilled serving bowls and hold them in the freezer while you repeat with the remaining frozen mixture. Garnish as you wish and serve immediately.

i knew you were coming so i baked a cake

136

# mango sorbet

**Makes 4 small servings**

*T*his recipe works even better in big batches.

**DO AHEAD:**

1. Place the sliced mangoes in the food processor or blender. Measure in the condensed milk and rum. Pulse until smooth and then freeze in the ice cube trays or storage container.

**TO FINISH:**

2. When the mixture is frozen, reprocess with a few quick pulses to break it up. Serve topped with some chopped pistachios.

**QUICK TIP:** You may be able to find mango slices already peeled in a sugar syrup in your produce section. Drain off the syrup, rinse to remove as much of the preservative taste as possible, and use these slices with the condensed milk and rum.

**VARIATION:** Use sliced ripe bananas (with or without the condensed milk) or papaya slices (with the condensed milk) and rum in the same proportions.

*2 mangoes, peeled and sliced, approximately 3 cups of fruit chunks, packed*

*½ cup condensed milk, full, low- or nonfat*

*¼ to ½ cup light rum*

*¼ cup shelled and coarsely chopped pistachios*

**EQUIPMENT**
paring knife; food processor or blender; plastic storage container or two ice-cube trays

frozen desserts

# semifreddo

*1 recipe Chocolate Mousse, Version I (page 152)*

*Chopped pecans, glacéed or candied fruits, or semisweet or white chocolate chips (optional)*

**EQUIPMENT**
9x4-inch loaf pan; plastic wrap; thin slicing knife

**Makes 8 to 10 servings**

Semifreddo is a rich version of homemade ice cream made without an ice cream maker. It can be prepared long before you need it, and leftovers become more dense the longer they dry out in the freezer. Who complains about dense, rich chocolate ice cream?

1. Line the bottom and sides of the loaf pan with plastic wrap, allowing enough extra wrap to cover the top completely.
2. Prepare the mousse at least a day or two before you expect company. Spoon the prepared mousse into the loaf pan, folding in any optional ingredients you choose, and smooth the top. Fold the flaps of plastic wrap over the top to cover completely and freeze until you are ready to serve.
3. When ready to serve, the pan will need a few minutes on the counter to soften enough for the wrap to be peeled away from the top of the mousse and used to lift the loaf out of the pan. Place a plate over the frozen mousse and invert onto a serving plate. Peel the wrap away from the sides and bottom.
4. With the knife, cut into ½-inch slices. (Running your knife blade under hot water will allow easy slicing.)

**QUICK TIP:** Be generous with the plastic wrap, and you'll have easy cleanup and no freezer smells or freezer burns.

# frozen bananas

Around my kitchen, if the bananas don't have any green on their skin, they are "too ripe"! What to do?

1. Freeze some in their skins to use for banana cakes.
2. Freeze some, peeled, sliced, and wrapped in plastic, to garnish ice cream sundaes, or to mash 1 cup with an ounce or two of rum into a fruit sorbet.
3. Peel, cut in half, and insert an ice cream stick or skewer. Immediately dip in melted semisweet chocolate and place in the freezer, to eat about 15 minutes later.

**VARIATION:**
See variation for Mango Sorbet, page 137.

**QUICK TIP:** To peel a frozen banana, give it a hot shower under running water in your sink for 10 seconds, then cut off the stem end and peel down using a sharp knife. Catch the inner skin fibers with the edge of the knife and scrape gently to the flesh. This way you don't have to wait until the banana defrosts in order to use it, and you keep most of the moisture in your mixture.

chapter eight

# puddings, mousses, and fools

vanilla pudding
rice pudding without the oven
tapioca pudding
bread pudding
chocolate chunk bread pudding
chocolate fudge pudding
fools
fruit mousse
chocolate mousse, version I
version II
booze mousse
true trifle
lemon curd
tiramisù, version I
version II
coeur à la crème
orange couscous with blueberries

When I was a child and my throat was sore, soothing comfort food came in the My-T-Fine box. That full-tummy feeling came in vanilla, chocolate, and butterscotch flavors, and the biggest treat was getting to lick the pot after the puddings were poured into bowls. Why not soothe yourself, from scratch, in just a few minutes, using your Pyrex cup, measuring spoons, and the microwave?

# ☙vanilla pudding

**Makes 2 servings, or a generous cake filling; doubled, enough for a 9-inch baked pie shell or a trifle**

*T*his *is a very thick, stable custard that can easily take on additional flavorings, nuts, or fruits; it is also thick enough to hold up for Boston Cream Pie (page 32) or Coconut Custard Pie (page 89). Flavored with liqueurs and lightened with whipped cream, it becomes a True Trifle (page 155) or Napoleon filling (page 199).*

1 cup milk (whole, low-fat, or nonfat)

1 tablespoon cornstarch

¼ cup sugar

¼ teaspoon salt

1 egg yolk

1 tablespoon butter

1 teaspoon vanilla extract

**EQUIPMENT**
2-cup Pyrex cup; 1-cup Pyrex cup; fork

## PROCEDURE FOR MICROWAVE:

1. Pour the milk into the 2-cup Pyrex measure and add the cornstarch, sugar, and salt. Stir with a fork to dissolve.

2. Microwave on High for 2 to 3 minutes. The mixture *must boil* to cook the cornstarch, but watch carefully to be sure that it doesn't boil over. Stir it down after this heating.

3. Put the egg yolk in the 1-cup Pyrex measure and *slowly* pour in half the milk mixture while mixing the egg with the fork. This tempers the egg, to avoid making scrambled eggs as you would if the hot milk hit the yolk suddenly.

4. Return this into the remaining hot milk mixture, stirring the hot milk with the fork as you pour in the egg-milk mixture. Then microwave on High for 1 or 2 minutes more; the mixture will begin to thicken.

5. Stir in the butter and vanilla. Cool in the measure to use in other recipes, or pour into serving dishes and refrigerate until serving.

**NOTE:** If you start with cold milk you may need an extra minute in the first heating step.

## PROCEDURE FOR SAUCEPAN:

1. Place the milk, cornstarch, sugar, and salt in the saucepan, set on medium heat, and stir constantly.

2. Put the egg yolk into the Pyrex cup and break it up with the fork.

3. Just as the milk is beginning to thicken (after perhaps 5 minutes of warming), pour ½ cup into the yolk, while mixing the yolk with your fork.

4. Incorporate the warmed yolk and milk into the saucepan mixture and be sure it comes to a boil to cook the cornstarch. *Keep stirring.*

**EQUIPMENT**
2-quart saucepan; mixing spoon; 1-cup Pyrex cup; fork

*puddings, mousses, and fools*

5. When bubbles appear all around your pan, remove it from the heat and add the butter and vanilla. Stir until smooth. This way takes about 10 minutes to prepare and leaves you with a pot to wash, but it tastes great and you get to lick the pot.

**NOTE:** This recipe doubles easily to make 4 servings or to fill a baked pie shell. If you make a double batch in the microwave, you must use a 1-quart Pyrex measure. Set on High for 2-minute intervals, checking to see when the pudding is as thick as you want it and the cornstarch has cooked off its raw, floury taste. The timing in the saucepan is just about the same.

**VARIATIONS:**
- Use ½ teaspoon of vanilla extract and ¼ teaspoon of almond extract for Almond Pudding, and top with coconut, banana, pecans, toasted almonds, or a sprinkling of **Praline** (page 130) just as you serve it.
- Whip 1 cup of heavy cream with 1 to 2 ounces of liqueur and fold into a cooled double recipe of pudding. This makes a wonderful velvety custard that is great in a True Trifle or for Napoleons (page 199).
- Pour the pudding into a gratin dish and sprinkle an even ¼-inch layer of dark brown sugar over the surface. Place directly under a preheated broiler to "brûlée" a topping in 2 to 5 minutes.
- For a more custardy rice pudding, prepare the recipe with ½ tablespoon cornstarch. After you add the butter and vanilla, add ½ cup cooked rice, 1 teaspoon orange zest, ¼ cup chopped dried fruits, or a swirl of ¼ cup **Dried Apricot Purée** (page 178) with a dollop of fresh **Whipped Cream**.

i knew you
were coming
so i baked a
cake

144

# rice pudding without the oven

**Makes 6 servings**

My mom always baked her rice pudding, but you don't have to turn on your oven for this recipe. A 2-quart saucepan does the job at a gentle simmer in less than half an hour.

1. Bring the milk, rice, sugar, and salt to a boil in the saucepan. Lower the heat and simmer, covered, for 15 to 20 minutes. Check to see if the rice is cooked to your preference.
2. Break the eggs into the Pyrex measure. Slowly pour ½ cup of the hot milk mixture into the eggs, stirring constantly. Pour the warmed eggs back into the saucepan, stirring constantly, and turn off the heat.
3. Stir in the vanilla and any optional ingredients and flavorings you select.
4. Allow to cool, off the heat, for 5 to 10 minutes. Serve warm or chilled, garnished with a sprinkle of cinnamon.

3 cups milk

½ cup raw white rice

¼ cup sugar

¼ teaspoon salt

2 eggs

1 teaspoon vanilla extract

½ cup raisins, currants, cranberries, or other dried fruits; ½ teaspoon cinnamon; ½ teaspoon lemon and/or orange zest; or ¼ teaspoon almond extract (optional)

**EQUIPMENT**
2-quart saucepan; 1-cup Pyrex cup; mixing spoon

puddings, mousses, and fools

# tapioca pudding

**Makes 4 to 6 servings**

2 eggs

2½ cups milk

3 tablespoons instant tapioca

¼ cup sugar

¼ teaspoon salt

1 teaspoon vanilla extract

**EQUIPMENT**
½-cup Pyrex bowl; fork; 2-quart saucepan; mixing spoon

*T*apioca comes from the root of the cassava plant. The large or small pearl textures are white in the box. Soaked, it softens, and as it cooks it becomes opaque, then clear and a bit chewy. As tapioca cooks, it thickens the custard around it, creating a delicately textured treat. I use instant tapioca, which needs no soaking and cooks more quickly.

Tapioca pudding is kid-friendly and easily digested, yet it can be dressed up for entertaining occasions.

1. Break the eggs into the Pyrex bowl and beat very lightly with the fork.
2. Place the milk, tapioca, sugar, salt, and eggs in the saucepan. Stir and simmer about 10 to 15 minutes, until the mixture begins to thicken and bubble. Stir in the vanilla. Serve warm or chilled.

**VARIATIONS:**
- Add 1 tablespoon butter at the end of cooking.
- Add 2 teaspoons instant espresso powder to the milk.
- Make a chocolate syrup swirl as the pudding cools in a serving bowl. Pour ½ cup chocolate syrup straight from the container and weave a pattern through the pudding. Or fill individual dessert bowls with the pudding and use 1 teaspoon to 1 tablespoon per portion.
- Swirl in softened dried fruits or **fruit purées** as the pudding is cooling in the serving bowl.
- On cold winter days, serve warm, topped with liqueur-flavored **Chantilly Cream** (page 69) in a heatproof mug.

**QUICK TIP:**   Instant tapioca is a great staple for the pantry. Try stirring 1 to 2 tablespoons around the fruit to thicken the juices released in a pie or a crisp or to give body to a saucy cooked compote.

i knew you were coming so i baked a **cake**

# bread pudding

**Makes 10 to 12 servings**

$H$*ere is a quick version of a classic dessert. You can be as virtuous or as decadent as you please. The recipe works well using any of these: 5 cups of half-and-half; 4 cups of low-fat milk and 1 cup heavy cream; 4 cups nonfat (skim) milk and 1 cup heavy cream; or 4 cups milk and 1 cup light cream to make the custard. While the almond extract is optional, it adds an extra dimension of flavor.*

¼ pound (1 stick) unsalted butter

Cooking spray (optional)

1 pound bread

1 cup raisins or golden raisins

1 cup sugar or Cinnamon-Sugar (page 22)

4 cups milk

1 cup light cream

6 eggs

2 teaspoons vanilla extract

⅛ teaspoon salt

½ teaspoon almond extract (optional)

**EQUIPMENT**
2-quart saucepan or 2-quart microwavable bowl; 9x13-inch (3-quart) baking pan or gratin pan; 3-quart mixing bowl; fork or whisk; 1-cup Pyrex cup
Optional: strainer

## DO AHEAD:

1. Use 1 tablespoon of the butter to grease the baking pan, or spray it with cooking spray.
2. Make several layers of bread in the pan, sprinkling raisins and a total of ¼ cup of the sugar between layers.
3. In the saucepan, bring the milk and cream (in whatever combination you like) to a boil, watching as it expands in the pot and forms a skin. Alternatively, microwave the milk and cream on High in the 2-quart bowl. The milk will climb the sides of the bowl, so you must allow plenty of room. Remove from the heat, cut in the butter to melt, and stir.
4. In the 3-quart mixing bowl, beat the eggs, the remaining ¾ cup sugar, the vanilla, salt, and optional almond extract with the fork or whisk.
5. Using the measuring cup, dip out ½ cup of the hot milk and drizzle it slowly into the eggs while beating them with the fork or whisk. You are trying to warm the eggs, not scramble them, so go slowly, gradually adding more milk.
6. When fully (even imperfectly!) combined, pour this custard onto and around the bread layered in the baking dish. (If you see scrambled eggs or pieces of congealed egg white, you can pour the custard through a strainer over the bread to remove those unattractive (but harmless and completely edible) pieces.

## TO FINISH:

7. You can bake this immediately or prepare it to this point, let the custard soak into the bread, and bake it an hour or two later. When you are ready, preheat the oven to 325°F. Bake the pudding for 45 to 60 minutes and serve warm with a dollop of **Chantilly Cream** (page 69).

puddings,
mousses,
and fools

**VARIATIONS:**

· An ounce or two of rum or brandy may be added to the custard.
· You can layer ½ cup **Dried Apricot Purée** (page 178) between the bread slices.
· An extra sprinkling of sugar or nuts on top just before baking will make a crunchy top.

# chocolate chunk bread pudding

**Makes 6 to 8 servings**

Cooking spray (optional)

2 cups milk

1 cup light cream

2 tablespoons unsalted butter

8 slices firm-textured bread, torn into pieces

3 eggs

½ cup sugar

1 teaspoon vanilla extract

¼ cup chocolate or coffee liqueur

1 ½ cups semisweet chocolate chunks or chips, OR ½ cup cocoa powder and ½ cup additional sugar

**EQUIPMENT**
8-inch square (2-quart) baking pan or gratin dish; 2-quart saucepan or 2-quart microwavable bowl; 1-cup Pyrex; fork

*H*ere is a rich and filling temptation to set before chocolate lovers. When served warm in large squares garnished with **Chantilly Cream** (page 69) this is indulgent enough, but drizzling warm Microwave Fudge Sauce (page 77) on top will give them a real thrill.

1. Preheat the oven to 325°F and grease the baking pan with cooking spray or an extra tablespoon of butter.
2. Scald the milk and cream in the saucepan or in the microwave on High in the 2-quart bowl. The milk will climb the sides of the bowl, so you must allow it room to expand. Remove from the heat and stir in the 2 tablespoons of butter until melted.
3. Tear the bread into the hot milk mix, stir together, and let stand 15 minutes to cool, so the eggs won't scramble when you mix them in.
4. Beat the eggs with the fork in the 1-cup Pyrex; add them and the sugar to the cooled bread mixture. Stir in the vanilla and liqueur and mix thoroughly.
5. Pour the mixture into the baking pan. Sprinkle the chocolate chips or cocoa mixture over the top. Bake 50 to 60 minutes until the top is puffed and set. Serve warm or chilled.

**VARIATIONS:**

This recipe works well using any of the following combinations: 3 cups of half-and-half; 2 cups of low-fat milk and 1 cup heavy cream; or 2 cups of nonfat (skim) milk and 1 cup heavy cream. Chocolate milk can replace the milk.

i knew you were coming so i baked a **cake**

148

# chocolate fudge pudding

**Makes 2 servings**

*T*his dark, dense pudding seems as if it should be terribly fattening, but if you try it with skim milk, no one will notice the missing butterfat. If it seems too dark, too fudgelike, you can cut the cocoa in half and still have a satisfying chocolate experience.

1 cup milk (whole, low-fat, or nonfat) or chocolate milk

2 tablespoons unsweetened cocoa

2 tablespoons sugar

1 tablespoon cornstarch

## EQUIPMENT
2-cup Pyrex cup; mixing spoon; 2-quart saucepan if not using microwave

## PROCEDURE FOR MICROWAVE:
1. Measure the ingredients directly into the Pyrex cup and stir; it will be a bit lumpy.
2. Microwave on High for 1 minute; stir to smooth.
3. Microwave again on High for 1 minute and stir. The pudding will "grow" in the cup and begin to thicken.
4. Microwave on High ½ to 1 minute more. It will be much thicker and will continue to thicken as it cools.

## PROCEDURE FOR SAUCEPAN:
Measure the ingredients into the saucepan and heat gently to a boil. Lower the temperature as it begins to grow in the pot; simmer and stir for 2 or 3 minutes to be sure that the cornstarch has cooked thoroughly and the pudding has begun to thicken. As it cools it will continue to thicken.

**QUICK TIP:** Fill an empty glass jar with these proportions of cocoa, sugar, and cornstarch, shake to mix them, and label it. Next time you want chocolate pudding, add 5 tablespoons of the mixture to 1 cup of milk, and proceed with the recipe.

## VARIATIONS:
· Double this recipe to fill a baked 9-inch pie shell. Top with **Whipped Cream** (page 68) and you have a lush chocolate pie.
· Stir 2 tablespoons confectioners' sugar into ½ cup tangy sour cream. Lightly swirl this into the pudding for a sophisticated flavor.
· If you like caramel with chocolate, layer **Dulce de Leche** (page 75) on a Chocolate Pie Crust (page 87), then top with this pudding.
· Add 1 tablespoon espresso powder for mocha pudding. This makes a terrific addition to Tiramisù (page 157) as well.

puddings, mousses, and fools

# fools

**Makes 4 to 6 servings**

1 cup heavy cream

1 teaspoon vanilla extract

2 tablespoons sugar

2 cups flavored
Whipped Cream

Cooked or puréed fruit such
as: 1 (12 ounce) package
frozen berries or sliced
peaches, defrosted and
drained, blended with ½ cup
raspberry jam; 1 recipe
Blueberry Sauce; or 1 recipe
Dried Apricot Purée (page
178) made with an extra ½
cup orange juice or enough
orange liqueur stirred in to
create a texture like applesauce

### EQUIPMENT
electric mixer or whisk and
3-quart bowl; mixing
spoon; tall serving glasses
such as parfait glasses, water goblets, or clear glass
bowls

*P*ick almost any fruit, cooked or frozen and thawed, puréed or chunky. Allow about 4 ounces per person. Pick up the heavy cream and off you go into a wonderful piece of culinary history. Serve as soon as possible to keep the billowing texture, but chill if the filled glasses must wait a bit. This is heady stuff.

1. Whip the heavy cream with the vanilla and sugar past the Chantilly stage, until it is firm.
2. Drop a rounded tablespoon of fruit on the bottom of a tall serving glass, then scoop in a layer of cream. Repeat the fruit, cream, fruit, cream to fill each glass.
3. Garnish with an extra berry, ½ teaspoon fruit purée, a sprig of mint, or a flower blossom.

### VARIATIONS:

The combination of **fruit purée** and **Whipped Cream** is light and rich at the same time. Let your imagination run wild—how about Gingered Whipped Cream (page 71) with mangoes? Or orange-flavored Whipped Cream (page 69) with Blueberry Sauce (page 177)? Chocolate Whipped Cream (page 70) with poached pears? The combinations are endless.

i knew you
were coming
so i baked a
cake

150

# fruit mousse

**Makes 6 servings**

*I*f you've mastered the previous recipe for fools, you can feel confident about tackling mousse. Here you include an envelope of gelatin and blend the fruit into the whipped cream. You can handle it!

## DO AHEAD:

1. Add the gelatin to ¼ cup boiling water in a ½-cup Pyrex bowl and stir with the fork to dissolve the grains. Add the lemon juice and stir.
2. Put the fruit in a 1-quart mixing bowl, add the softened gelatin, and the optional lemon zest and liqueur, and blend.
3. In the 2-quart mixing bowl, whip the cream and sugar past the Chantilly stage until it is firm and holds a shape. (You may want to set aside about 1 cup of the whipped cream at this point, to use as a garnish later on.)
4. Gently fold the fruit mixture into the cream and chill the mousse in a serving bowl, a baked pie shell, or in individual portions.

## TO FINISH:

5. Garnish each serving with a dollop of extra whipped cream and a sliced fresh strawberry or a heaping tablespoon of loose blueberries, raspberries, or blackberries for contrast.

**NOTE:** This mousse can also be poured directly into a cake-lined mold, where it will conform to the shape of the container. See the recipe for a Bombe in Pound Cake Combinations on page 193.

1 envelope plain gelatin

Juice of 1 lemon, approximately 1 ounce

12 ounces fruit such as: frozen raspberries, blueberries, peaches, or strawberries; or 1½ cups of Berry Purée (page 176), Blueberry Sauce (page 177), the variations of Blueberry Sauce using fresh peaches, nectarines, or plums, or Dried Apricot Purée (page 178)

½ cup sugar

1 cup heavy cream, plus additional for garnish if you wish

Zest of 1 lemon (to be added to the fruit) (optional)

¼ cup orange liqueur (optional)

### EQUIPMENT
½-cup Pyrex bowl; fork; 1-quart mixing bowl; electric mixer or whisk; 2-quart mixing bowl; curved rubber spatula; serving bowl or pie shell or individual serving glasses

puddings,
mousses,
and fools

# chocolate mousse

*A mousse always requires time to become firm. Thus, it is a great company dessert because it must be prepared well ahead of time and will simply need a final garnish before serving.*

## version I: with eggs and cream

**Makes 8 to 10 servings**

2 cups (12 ounces) semisweet chocolate, chopped in 1-inch pieces, or 2 cups semisweet chocolate chips

¼ pound (1 stick) unsalted butter

6 egg yolks

½ cup sugar

¼ cup liqueur of your choice (coffee, orange, and raspberry all complement chocolate)

1 pint heavy cream

**EQUIPMENT**
2-cup Pyrex cup or 1-quart mixing bowl; 2-quart saucepan; 2-quart mixing bowl; electric mixer or whisk; 3-quart mixing bowl

1. Melt the chocolate and butter in the Pyrex cup for 30 seconds in the microwave on Medium-Low, stir, and microwave again for 15 seconds at a time and stir, repeating until the mixture is melted and smooth. Alternatively, set the butter and chocolate in the 1-quart mixing bowl over the 2-quart saucepan containing 1 inch of simmering water. Melt and set aside to cool.

2. Combine the egg yolks, sugar, and liqueur in the 2-quart bowl and warm over the simmering water in the 2-quart saucepan. Stir constantly while heating. Rub a drop between your fingers to feel if the sugar granules are dissolved. When the egg mixture becomes thick and lighter in color and the sugar has dissolved, remove from the heat and whip the yolk mixture until cooled and thicker still.

3. In the 3-quart mixing bowl, beat the cream until it holds its shape.

4. Fold the cooled chocolate into the whipped yolks and then fold the whipped cream into the chocolate-egg mixture.

5. Pour into a large serving bowl or individual dishes and chill.

**NOTE:** See "Frozen Desserts" to make this into Semifreddo (page 138).

# version II: eggs only, no cooking

**Makes 8 to 10 servings**

*T*his is the fail-safe method. If double-boilers strike fear in your heart, but you can set up the mixer and a timer while you're taking care of ten other tasks, then this is the mousse for you. It makes a delicious pie, garnished with whipped cream and chopped nuts.

1. In the large bowl of an electric mixer, cream the butter and sugar.
2. Melt the chocolate in the Pyrex cup in the microwave at Medium-Low for 15 seconds. Stir and repeat heating until the chocolate is melted.
3. Add the melted chocolate and vanilla to the creamed mixture and combine. Add one egg at a time, beating 5 minutes on a medium setting after each addition, for a total beating time of 20 minutes. The beating time binds the ingredients for this mousse, and it makes the mousse strong enough to hold up in a pie.
4. Pour the mousse into a serving bowl or individual dishes, or spread evenly in a baked pie shell. Chill at once. Garnish with Chantilly Cream (page 69) and a sprinkling of nuts.

**NOTE:**  As these eggs are uncooked, there is some concern regarding salmonella. Use the freshest eggs, chill the mousse immediately, and eat it chilled. Anyone who is pregnant, or who has a sensitivity to eggs, an easily upset stomach, or a compromised immune system, should use the mousse version on page 152 instead of this one.

½ pound (2 sticks) unsalted butter, softened

1 ½ cups sugar

4 squares unsweetened chocolate, melted and cooled, or 4 (1-ounce) pre-melted packets

2 teaspoons vanilla extract

4 eggs

1 recipe Nick Malgieri's No-Roll Pie Crust (page 86) (optional)

Whipped cream and/or chopped walnuts or pecans, for garnish

**EQUIPMENT**
electric mixer; 3-quart mixing bowl; 1-cup Pyrex cup

puddings,
mousses,
and fools

# booze mousse

**Makes 4 to 6 servings**

1 envelope plain gelatin

¼ cup lemon juice (2 lemons)

¼ cup sugar

½ cup Scotch whiskey

1 cup sour cream

chocolate shavings, frozen cherries, or berries (optional)

**EQUIPMENT**
2-cup Pyrex cup; fork or whisk

*A*ll out of just about everything? There's still something you can make. You can purchase six dessert shells, or mound this in four tall glasses to serve with plain cookies.

1. Sprinkle the gelatin into ¼ cup boiling water in the Pyrex cup and stir with the fork to loosen and dissolve the granules. Add the lemon juice, sugar, and Scotch, stirring to combine. Blend in the sour cream with the fork or whisk.
2. Pour into 4 individual tall glasses or 1 bowl to chill at least 2 hours. When set, scoop into dessert shells and garnish with chocolate shavings, frozen and drained cherries, or some berries.

**NOTE:** This mousse can also be poured into an attractive mold that has been sprayed with cooking spray. Chill and unmold carefully onto a serving platter.

# true trifle

**Makes about 2 quarts**

*T*his classic is made of three elements: a light cake, a custard, and fruit. It can be made ahead of time and adapts easily to different combinations of fruits, cake, and liqueur flavors.

**DO AHEAD:**

1. Make the pudding and chill until it is cool to the touch. Hold it in the refrigerator in the 1-quart Pyrex cup or a 1-quart mixing bowl, covered with plastic wrap spread on the pudding's surface.

**TO FINISH:**

2. In the 3-quart mixing bowl, whip the cream, vanilla, and ¼ cup of the sugar to soft peaks, just past the **Chantilly** stage (see page 69).
3. Fold half the whipped cream into the cooled pudding.
4. In the 2-quart bowl, toss the berries with the remaining ¾ cup sugar and the liqueur.
5. Place a layer of ladyfingers or cake on the bottom of a serving bowl, preferably a pretty glass one so the layers may be seen. Layer half the lightened pudding onto the cake layer, top with half the berry mixture, and add another layer of ladyfingers or cake. Repeat these layers and top with the remaining whipped cream.
6. Chill the Trifle and serve enormous spoonfuls directly from the bowl, garnished with some extra berries if you like.

**QUICK TIP:**   You can make the vanilla pudding a day or two ahead of time and assemble this Trifle the day before company is coming. The fruit juices may bleed into the custard but the flavors will mellow. Do not garnish until the last minute.

**NOTE:**   Slices of mango, papaya, frozen and thawed peaches, or cherries can add different accents to a trifle. All blend well with the traditional berries.

Double recipe Vanilla Pudding (page 143)

2 cups heavy cream

1 teaspoon vanilla extract

1 cup confectioners' sugar

1 package ladyfingers (at least 2 dozen pieces), or 1 pound of pound cake, angel cake, or sponge cake, sliced

4 to 6 cups fresh or thawed frozen mixed berries, using the juice

¼ to ½ cup raspberry, orange, or black currant liqueur

Extra fresh berries for garnish (optional)

**EQUIPMENT**
electric mixer or whisk and 2- and 3-quart mixing bowls; 1-quart Pyrex cup or mixing bowl; plastic wrap; glass-sided 2-quart serving bowl

puddings, mousses, and fools

# ❧lemon curd

**Makes about 14 ounces, a little more than 1½ cups**

*Juice and zest of 4 to 5 lemons (about ½ cup juice and about 2 teaspoons zest)*

*6 egg yolks*

*1 cup sugar*

*¼ pound (1 stick) unsalted butter, cut into ½-inch chunks*

**EQUIPMENT**
grater or zester and paring knife; juicer or fork; 1-cup Pyrex cup; 2-quart stainless or other nonreactive saucepan (no aluminum or iron!); mixing spoon; 1-quart mixing bowl; wax paper; plastic wrap
Optional: Only if necessary, a strainer

*I* imagined that this recipe might be the hardest in this book, but it's not. Its saving graces are how easily the procedure breaks into two parts, how well it keeps in the refrigerator (for weeks!), and how it works in so many dessert combinations. Suggestions for its use appear throughout this book.

**DO AHEAD:**

1. Zest the lemons onto a sheet of wax paper and juice the lemons into a Pyrex cup.

**TO FINISH:**

2. Separate the eggs, dropping the yolks into the saucepan (and the whites into a plastic storage container to label and freeze for another dessert).

3. Add the sugar and lemon juice to the yolks and cook on medium-low heat for 10 to 12 minutes, until thickened. You must stir *constantly* and warm this mixture *gently* to avoid curdling. (If you have gone too fast or stepped away, you can rescue your curd by straining it before you proceed to the next step.)

4. Remove the pan from the heat. Stir in the butter chunks until melted and then add the lemon zest.

5. Transfer to the mixing bowl to cool, then place plastic wrap directly on the surface of the curd and chill.

**QUICK TIP:** While you have the grater and juicer out, make some extra zest and juice to store in the freezer and you have a start on several other recipes.

i knew you were coming so i baked a **cake**

# tiramisù

*This dessert tastes best when you let the flavors blend overnight, but if you must serve it immediately, no one will complain. You can't miss with either version here. Both recipes double easily if you expect a large crowd.*

## tiramisù I

**Makes one 9x4 loaf pan, 4 servings**

**DO AHEAD:**

1. Blend together the cream cheese and cream until smooth, or stir the honey into the ricotta.

**TO ASSEMBLE:**

2. Open the ladyfingers or slice the pound cake ⅜ inch thick. Cover the bottom of the loaf pan with cake. Moisten the cake with half the liqueur.
3. Pour on the cool pudding and spread evenly. Layer on the rest of the ladyfingers or cake and moisten with the remaining liqueur.
4. Spread the top with the cream cheese or ricotta mixture. Garnish with shaved chocolate or mini chips and sprinkle with cinnamon or cocoa powder.

**NOTE:**   The food processor will chop small chunks or chips of chocolate in 10 seconds for this garnish, or you can use a swivel-bladed vegetable peeler or grater to shave some bits off a chocolate bar. Whichever finishing look and texture you prefer, the real taste is in the layers.

1 recipe Chocolate Fudge or Mocha Pudding (variation, page 149)

¼ pound cream cheese or mascarpone[†]

¼ cup heavy cream[†]

½ pound pound cake or 12 to 16 ladyfingers

¼ cup coffee liqueur or chocolate liqueur, or more to taste

Shaved chocolate, mini chocolate chips, cinnamon, and/or cocoa powder for garnish (optional)

**EQUIPMENT**
9x4-inch loaf pan; 1-quart mixing bowl

[†]1 cup ricotta cheese mixed with 2 tablespoons honey may be used to replace the heavy cream and cream cheese.

puddings, mousses, and fools

# tiramisù II

**Makes 8 to 10 servings**

1 pound plain, marbled, or chocolate pound cake

½ pound mascarpone or cream cheese

1 cup confectioners' sugar

1 teaspoon vanilla extract

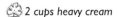2 cups heavy cream

¼ cup coffee or chocolate liqueur, or more to taste

3 cups espresso or strong coffee

¼ teaspoon cocoa or cinnamon, or 1 teaspoon chocolate shavings, for garnish

**EQUIPMENT**
electric mixer or whisk and 3-quart mixing bowl; paring knife; 8-inch square or 9x13-inch pan; 1-quart Pyrex or 1-quart mixing bowl; pastry brush or tablespoon

1. Slice the cake to ⅜-inch-thick pieces and set aside.
2. Whip the mascarpone or cream cheese about 2 minutes in the electric mixer. Add the sugar and vanilla to the cheese and whip until smooth. Pour the heavy cream into the cheese and whip until it is fully incorporated.
3. Combine the liqueur and coffee in the 1-quart Pyrex cup.
4. If using an 8-inch square pan, line the pan with a third of the cake slices and moisten with a third of the coffee mixture. If using a 9x13 pan, use half the cake slices and half the coffee mixture. For the 8-inch pan, layer a third of the cheese mixture onto the cake: for the 9x13 pan, use half the cheese mixture. Then repeat the layering of cake, coffee, and cheese twice more for the 8-inch pan, and once more for the 9x13 pan, ending with cheese on top.
5. Garnish with a sprinkle of cocoa powder, cinnamon, or chocolate shavings.

i knew you were coming so i baked a **cake**

# coeur à la crème

An elegant dessert, this is also a wonderful accompaniment to tea or an afternoon snack with plain or sweet crackers. It's a great conversation starter, a bit different from the usual cheese board. During the spring and summer it is terrific with berries, and in fall and winter I serve it with crystallized ginger.

1. Measure the cottage cheese, cream cheese, sour cream, and sugar into the 3-quart mixing bowl and blend until smooth, preferably with an electric mixer.
2. In the 2-quart bowl, whip the cream just past the billowing Chantilly stage, until it doubles in volume. Fold it and 1 tablespoon of the ginger, if using, gently into the cheese mixture.
3. Line the strainer, basket, or special coeur à la crème mold with the cheesecloth and fill with the mixture. Fold the cheesecloth over the cheese mixture. Set over a tray or bowl in the refrigerator overnight; the whey will seep out through the lining.
4. To unmold, hold the edges of the lining away from the top surface of the form, invert onto a serving plate, and carefully peel away the cheesecloth.
5. If you used ginger, garnish the top with the second tablespoon. Or garnish with fresh berries and serve the Strawberry Sauce on the side.

**NOTE:** Special molds (often heart-shaped) for this dessert have holes in the bottom to permit drainage of whey. You will find them at kitchensupply shops.

1 cup cottage cheese

½ pound cream cheese

1 cup sour cream

¼ cup confectioners' sugar

½ cup heavy cream

2 tablespoons chopped crystallized ginger, Berry Purée (page 176), or Strawberry Sauce variation (page 167) and fresh strawberries (optional)

**EQUIPMENT**
electric mixer or whisk; 2- and 3-quart mixing bowls; a coeur à la crème mold with drainage holes or a strainer or a 6-inch basket; cheesecloth, a cotton handkerchief or a napkin to line the mold; a tray or bowl to set the mold onto in the refrigerator

puddings, mousses, and fools

# orange couscous with blueberries

**Makes about 4 cups, serving 6 to 8**

2 cups raw couscous

½ teaspoon salt

2 cups orange juice

1 teaspoon orange zest, 1 or 2 oranges

2 oranges, peeled and cut into segments (see instructions in Macerated Oranges, page 169), or 1 can mandarin orange segments, well drained

1 pint fresh blueberries or dried cranberries

**EQUIPMENT**
2-quart mixing bowl; zester or grater; paring knife

*This* sweet couscous is great as a dessert after a meal of Mediterranean flavors, for a summer buffet, or for a late-afternoon snack.

1. In the mixing bowl, combine the couscous and salt with 2 cups boiling water. Stir to moisten all the grains, then let stand 2 minutes.
2. Add the orange juice 1 cup at a time, stirring, and then allow the couscous to absorb the liquid for about 10 minutes.
3. Taste the couscous, adding more juice if the grains still seem hard, and more salt if you like. Add the orange zest and segments and stir the couscous. Add the berries and stir just before serving. Serve at room temperature.

chapter 9

# fruit fare

sautéed apples
baked apples
apple purée
sautéed bananas
broiled bananas

## uncooked fruit compotes

strawberries in orange liqueur
pineapples in rum
macerated oranges
mangoes in white wine
compote combinations
brandied fruit, or rumtuffle

## cooked fruit compotes

dried fruit compote
loose grapes
pears in port

## fruit purées and sauces

berry purée
blueberry sauce
dried apricot purée
date purée
prune purée

Fruit desserts are always appreciated, no matter how calorie-conscious, cholesterol-conscious, or finicky your guests may be. The simpler the preparation, the better. Serve with a butter cookie or plain cake; you'll always score a hit.

# sautéed apples

**Makes 2 servings**

*T*his simplest of all desserts is my son's all-time favorite, even ahead of Granny's Oatmeal Cookies! Whenever I count his five fruits and vegetables for the day and come up short, I offer to make him a special, personal batch. It's an easy sell.

1. Peel and core the apples and slice them from stem to blossom end about ¼ inch thick.

2. Heat 1 tablespoon of the butter in the pan and add one-quarter of the apple slices. Do not crowd the pan. Each piece must be in contact with the bottom of the pan so it will brown and hold firm. (If you stuff them all in you will make applesauce—not a problem, but not the result you're looking for.) When one side browns, remove it to a serving plate, setting it browned side up. Repeat layer by layer, adding ½ tablespoon more butter as needed.

3. Add the sugar and optional ingredients to the pan only with the last layer. As the sugar melts it will turn brown, or caramelize, and will make a light glaze to top the apples. Or just sprinkle Cinnamon-Sugar (page 22) on the apples as they cool on the serving plate. Serve warm, with cookies or ice cream if you like, or heaped onto a puff pastry shell. These also make a delicious filling for **Crêpes** (page 53).

2 apples, preferably Granny Smith, greening, or Golden Delicious

2 or 3 tablespoons butter

1 tablespoon sugar

¼ teaspoon cinnamon, 2 tablespoons raisins or currants, 1 tablespoon rum or orange liqueur (for grownups only), or 1 tablespoon lemon juice (optional)

**EQUIPMENT**
paring knife; 8-inch nonstick sauté pan; spatula; serving plate

fruit
fare

# baked apples

**Makes 6 servings**

*6 Rome Beauty or other large apples*

*6 tablespoons Cinnamon-Sugar (page 22)*

*1 cup softened dried fruit (raisins, cranberries, currants, cherries) or Macaroon Topping (page 67), or Berry Purée (page 176) for really blushing beauties, optional*

**EQUIPMENT**
9x13-inch baking dish, large enough to hold the apples upright; vegetable peeler or paring knife; apple corer

A wide range of apples are at their freshest and best in the fall. While available year round thanks to preservation and refrigeration techniques, the very best apples have experienced the very least handling: picked, packed, and eaten.

Year round I choose greenings or Granny Smiths for most apple recipes, but to bake, the softer and sweeter varieties such as Rome Beauties are preferable. So, having chosen good apples, dress them, stuff them, and bake.

1. Preheat the oven to 350°F.
2. Wash and core the applies and peel a strip around the shoulders or mid-section to allow for expansion during baking. Sprinkle with Cinnamon-Sugar. Fill the cavity with your choice of filling or leave it empty for faster baking.
3. Pour 1 cup of water into the bottom of a 9x13 baking pan so the apples won't stick or burn, and the juices will caramelize to produce a syrup. Bake about 45 minutes, preferably while guests are eating dinner, so the apples will be warm, fresh from the oven, for dessert. Garnish with crème fraîche, frozen yogurt, or Caramel Sauce (page 73) and they won't last long.

**NOTE:** If you like baked apples, try baking pears, cored and crowned with Macaroon Topping (page 67).

i knew you
were coming
so i baked a
cake

164

# apple purée

**Makes about 1½ cups as purée; about ¾ cup as apple butter**

*B*ig baskets of apples always beckon to me in the fall. Somehow, I always buy more than we'll eat, or someone presents me with more than we can eat that month. So I freeze pint batches of applesauce for times when I just want to defrost a homemade dessert to offer with some cookies.

*4 apples of your choice (I prefer Granny Smiths)*

*Juice of 1 lemon (about 1 ounce) (optional)*

*2 teaspoons sugar or Cinnamon-Sugar (page 22), or more to taste*

**EQUIPMENT**
2-quart saucepan; paring knife

1. Peel and core the apples and cut them into eighths (sixteenths if you're in a hurry). Put them in the saucepan with the optional lemon juice and the sugar. Cover and set on low heat.

2. Check and stir in about 3 to 5 minutes, adding water 2 tablespoons at a time if the apples are not giving off moisture and seem to be browning quickly. Check every 5 minutes, stirring and breaking up the apple chunks. Some varieties of apple, such as Rome Beauties, break up faster than Granny Smiths or greenings, so you have to check them.

3. For chunky apple sauce, cook 15 to 20 minutes. For apple purée, smoother in consistency and slightly more caramelized, cook 20 to 25 minutes. To make apple butter, continue to cook, uncovered, at very low heat, after the purée stage until you reach a drier, browned, thicker consistency, about 35 to 40 minutes all together. Be careful of "spitting" at this stage; the heat causes the purée to jump out of the pot, messing up the stovetop and giving nasty spot-burns if you are too close. Pull the pot off the heat to give a quick stir, so the bottom won't scorch, and tip the pot slightly away from yourself, so you won't be burned. The stovetop cleans up pretty quickly at the end.

fruit fare

# sautéed bananas

**Makes 2 servings as a dessert, 4 servings as a topping**

2 bananas

Juice of 1 lemon, approximately 1 ounce

1 tablespoon butter

¼ cup dark brown sugar

Raisins or currants (optional)

1 or 2 ounces rum (optional)

**EQUIPMENT**
paring knife; 8-inch non-stick sauté pan; spatula

*Quick, easy, and great to serve with butter cookies, on pound cake, or with ice cream. Lemon juice keeps the bananas from browning, prevents the sugar from crystallizing, and helps make a sauce, so be generous with it.*

1. Peel and cut the bananas into diagonal coins and immediately squirt half the lemon juice on the cut surfaces to prevent browning.
2. Melt the butter in the pan. When the butter is bubbly but not yet brown, add the sliced bananas. Cook 2 or 3 minutes on Medium-High. Turn and cook 2 minutes more, adding the sugar, the remaining lemon juice, and the optional fruit and rum. Serve immediately, while warm and fragrant.

# broiled bananas

**Makes 4 servings**

4 bananas

¼ cup banana or orange liqueur, or rum

¼ cup dark brown sugar

**EQUIPMENT**
paring knife; baking pan or gratin pan

*Desserts don't come much faster or simpler than this one. Pineapple or mango slices are also wonderful with this brown sugar glaze broiled on top. You can cut them ahead of time, topping with the brown sugar just before broiling. Adding extra liqueur to the pan after broiling enhances the flavor and amount of the sauce. Serve with scoops of ice cream or frozen yogurt and plain cookies.*

1. Preheat the broiler.
2. Peel and slice the bananas into diagonal coins and arrange them overlapping in the pan. Douse with the liqueur. Crumble the brown sugar on top and immediately place directly under the broiler, as close as you can, for 3 to 5 minutes, watching carefully.

*My mother always called this fruit salad. Then I learned that Aunt Marian added a few drops of lemon juice to prevent browning, and sugar to make more syrup. Then my mother-in-law showed me the orange liqueur she used when she cut up fruits hours before company came, and it never browned. Then I decided I liked single fruits or more limited combinations. What's your preference?*

## strawberries in orange liqueur

**Makes 4 to 6 servings**

*I prefer this prepared the day it will be used, but by the next day you will have a very tasty strawberry sauce for ice cream sundaes, strawberry shortcake, strawberry Fool (page 150), Coeur à la Crème (page 159), or sliced pound cake. Freeze extra, if there is any.*

**DO AHEAD:** Rinse the berries. Save 6 of the largest, most perfect berries for garnish. Stem and slice the rest of the berries into the mixing bowl. Sprinkle on the sugar and liqueur. Toss and allow to macerate for 1 hour or more.

**QUICK TIP:** To make strawberry fans: Leave the stems on the berries and make several cuts up from the points to the shoulders, then press down gently at the shoulders to spread the slices apart.

**VARIATION:**

Strawberry Sauce:

To make a sauce for an ice cream sundae, put the mixture into the food processor and pulse about 10 times. You can stir 1 tablespoon cornstarch into ¼ cup orange juice or water, bring it to a boil, then stir this into the Strawberry Sauce to thicken it if you want more body.

2 pints strawberries

¼ cup granulated sugar or confectioners' sugar, which dissolves more rapidly

¼ cup orange-flavored liqueur

**EQUIPMENT**
paring knife; 2-quart mixing bowl

fruit
fare

# pineapples in rum

1 ripe pineapple

¼ cup light rum or orange-flavored liqueur

¼ cup confectioners' sugar (optional)

**EQUIPMENT**
cutting board; chef's knife; 2-quart serving bowl

**Makes 4 to 6 servings**

**DO AHEAD:**

1. Slice the top off the pineapple and reserve to garnish the serving plate. Slice down the sides and bottom of the pineapple, removing the skin and all brown nodules on the fruit. Find the central core and slice down next to it on opposite sides, then slice the remaining fruit into wedges ¼ inch thick. Place the pieces in the bowl with as much juice as you can capture.

2. Pour the liqueur (and optional sugar) on top and allow the pineapple to macerate several hours or overnight in the refrigerator. This mellows and improves with time, as long as there is enough liqueur to cover the fruit, so it will not brown. Serve as a light finish to a meal or with Mango Sorbet (page 137).

i knew you were coming so i baked a **cake**

# macerated oranges

**Makes 4 to 6 servings**

**DO AHEAD:**

1. Spread the coconut on foil and toast under the broiler or in the toaster oven for about 3 minutes. Stir around and toast a bit longer if you like your coconut with more color. (I prefer the broadest range from pure white to crispy dark brown, as accents for the oranges.) Set aside to cool.

2. Peel the oranges through the skin and membrane beneath. To cut into pieces, the simplest way is to slice the oranges across the segments about ⅜ inch thick. For a skill challenge, "supreme" the orange segments by running the paring knife along the membranes and removing the juicy wedges; squeeze any juice remaining near the white membrane and discard the membranes.

3. Arrange the orange slices or segments in the serving plate. Sprinkle on the sugar and liqueur and allow the oranges to macerate an hour or more before serving.

**TO FINISH:**

4. Top with the coconut just at serving time, so the contrasts of color and texture will be clearest, and the coconut, crisp.

¼ cup shredded coconut

6 to 8 navel oranges

¼ cup confectioners' sugar

¼ cup orange-flavored liqueur

**EQUIPMENT**
aluminum foil; paring knife; cutting board; 2-quart serving plate that can hold the juices

# mangoes in white wine

**Makes 4 servings**

**W**hile mangoes are in season, it makes sense to cut up some extras to freeze for a Mango-Molasses Upside-Down Cake (page 36). Small pieces work well as a layer for True Trifle (page 155) or you can purée for Mango Sorbet (page 137).

**DO AHEAD:** Peel and slice the mangoes. Sprinkle sugar on top and douse with white wine. Allow to macerate several hours or overnight in the refrigerator. Freeze any leftovers; I'm sure you'll find a use for them.

2 medium or larger mangoes

1 tablespoon sugar

¼ cup white wine

**EQUIPMENT**
paring knife; cutting board; 1-quart serving bowl

fruit fare

169

# compote combinations

*Here are some of my favorite combinations. The colors and contrasts of these combinations call for just a simple cookie to complete dessert.*

· Chunks of cantaloupe, honeydew, watermelon and/or other varieties of melon, and pineapple, enhanced with a sprinkle of sugar and rum or melon-flavored liqueur.
· Mixed berries sprinkled with sugar. (Let the mixture sit for an hour or so to release the syrup.)
· Berries with peeled, diced pears. Sugar the berries and they will release their juices to color the pears if you toss and stir once or twice before serving.
· Orange segments with strawberries, sugar, and orange liqueur.
· Several different kinds of melon with grapes of contrasting colors.

i knew you
were coming
so i baked a
cake

170

# brandied fruit, or rumtuffle

*T*his treat must be the reason large-mouth jars exist. Traditional recipes tell you to start about a year ahead. Sugar and brandy are combined with cut-up fruits in season and left to steep. More sugar, brandy, and fruit are added as the seasons pass. (You can start this the day before you plan to serve it, and keep it going as long as you like.)

Keep the big jar in a cool place; there's no need to refrigerate it. Pineapple, loose seedless grapes, cherries, apricots, nectarines, peaches, plums, pears, mangoes, and berries are all wonderful. It's always great with pound cake and ice cream, for topping crêpes, or just as it is. Dip in as deep as you can to reach for your favorites (they're always at the bottom), and while you're at it, you're stirring the pot. Use the following proportions in whatever quantities suit you.

1 cup fruit-flavored or regular brandy

1 cup sugar

2 cups cut and cleaned fruits

**EQUIPMENT**
wide-mouthed jar, quart-size or larger

1. Pour brandy and sugar into the jar, close tightly, and shake to dissolve the sugar. Add cut and cleaned fruits and shake again to be sure the fruit is coated.
2. Allow the fruits to macerate overnight or longer—this keeps mellowing with time, and the flavors will blend and improve. You can continue to add to this bottle, refreshing the brandy to be sure it covers all the fruit you add, and adding sugar so you'll have a wonderful syrup.

fruit
fare

*I always keep dried fruits in the pantry. When gently simmered, they readily take on the flavors of whole cinnamon sticks, cloves, cardamom pods, or liqueurs, becoming a healthful addition to pies, tarts, pudding, or a quick trifle. A whirl in the food processor with some extra liquid and you have a sauce or cake filling.*

# dried fruit compote

**Makes 3 to 4 cups**

*1 pound dried apricots*

*½ pound raisins, golden raisins, or currants*

*2 to 3 cups orange juice*

*Orange-flavored liqueur, light rum, fortified wine such as marsala or sherry, or port (optional)*

**EQUIPMENT**
1-quart Pyrex cup
Optional: Paring knife or kitchen shears

**PROCEDURE FOR MICROWAVE:**

1. If you want the apricots in smaller pieces, cut or snip them up before you begin cooking. Place the apricots and raisins in the Pyrex cup and add orange juice to cover the fruit.

2. Microwave on High for 2 minutes. Stir to be sure no fruit is burning. Microwave on High, 1 minute at a time until the medley is soft. The juice will be absorbed and will thicken as the fruits release their sugars.

3. Remove from the microwave and let cool. The compote will thicken further as it cools. If you like, add liqueur as the mixture is cooling.

**PROCEDURE FOR SAUCEPAN:**

Combine and simmer everything in a 1-quart saucepan, covered, for about 10 minutes, until softened.

**NOTE:** Serve this as a condiment with ham, turkey, or veal dinners or as an accompaniment to a simple cake or cookies. Warm or chilled, it's a friendly touch.

**OTHER GREAT COMBINATIONS:**

· 1 cup each apricots and prunes, softened in 2 cups of orange juice, with zest and juice of 1 lemon added after the fruit has been cooked.

· 1 cup each dried cherries, raisins, and cranberries, softened in 2 cups of orange or apple juice, with 2 tablespoons chopped crystallized ginger added after the fruit has been cooked.

i knew you were coming so i baked a **cake**

- 2 cups prunes and 1 cup cranberries with ½ teaspoon ground cardamom or 2 or 3 whole cardamom pods, softened in 2 cups of cranberry juice or water, with the zest of 1 lemon added after the fruit has been cooked.
- 1 cup figs, ½ cup raisins, and 1 cup apricots with a cinnamon stick, softened in 2 cups of apple juice laced with ¼ cup of brandy.
- ½ cup each dried strawberries, blueberries, and golden raisins, softened in 1 cup of water, then laced with ¼ cup of orange liqueur after the fruit has been cooked.

# loose grapes

**Makes about 1½ cups cooked sauce**

*2½ cups seedless grapes, stemmed and washed*

*¼ cup sugar*

*1 teaspoon cornstarch*

**EQUIPMENT**
1-quart Pyrex cup and plastic wrap, or 2-quart saucepan; mixing spoon

W*hat do you do with the grapes that fall off the stems? And the ones left on the stem after someone has picked at them? Toss them into Rumtuffle (page 171), or make a sauce to use up soon or freeze until you want to make a fool, a trifle, or a cooked fruit compote.*

**PROCEDURE FOR MICROWAVE:**

1. Place the grapes, sugar, and cornstarch in the Pyrex cup, stir to coat the grapes with the sugar and cornstarch, and cover with plastic wrap.
2. Microwave on High for 3 minutes.
3. Remove from the microwave. Open carefully so the steam rises away from your face. Stir and rewrap.
4. Microwave on High for 2 more minutes, until the contents are bubbly. Some grapes remain whole, while others will have broken down and made a sauce with the sugar and cornstarch. This sauce *must come to a full boil* so the cornstarch will boil clear and then thicken as it cools. It may need a third round of heating.
5. Remove from the microwave, stir, and allow to cool, then use alone or in combination with peaches or berries.

**PROCEDURE FOR SAUCEPAN:**   Combine the ingredients in a saucepan and simmer 10 to 15 minutes, until the mixture comes to a full, bubbly boil to dissolve and cook the cornstarch and thicken the sauce. Cool before using.

**NOTE:**   See also Rhubarb Pie, page 96, for another quick compote idea.

i knew you were coming so i baked a **cake**

# pears in port

**4 to 6 servings**

*P*ort makes a thick, tawny-colored sauce. Choose firm to slightly unripe pears rather than very soft, bruised fruits. Anjous and Bartletts work well, and tiny Seckels in season are great for a dessert buffet, when everyone wants to taste everything. The proportions here are enough for 4 to 6 standard pears or 10 to 15 Seckel pears.

4 to 6 pears, or 10 to 15 Seckel pears

1 lemon, cut in half

1 cup port for 4 to 6 pears

¼ cup sugar

**EQUIPMENT**
2-quart saucepan; vegetable peeler or apple corer; paring knife; rubber spatula; serving plate that can hold the sauce

1. Starting ½ inch down from the stem, peel the pears all around, leaving the stem untouched. From the bottom (blossom) end, use a vegetable peeler or apple corer to remove the seeds. Cut a thin slice off the bottom of each pear so they will stand up in the pot.
2. Stand the pears in the saucepan, squeeze the lemon juice on their peeled sides, then put the lemons in the pan with the port, sugar, and water to cover. Bring to a boil, covered.
3. Lower the heat and simmer, covered, for 10 to 15 minutes, then check for tenderness by inserting the paring knife into the bottom of one pear. Keep cooking if the pears seem too hard. When they are tender, remove with the rubber spatula to the serving dish.
4. Uncover the pot and reduce the sauce over high heat until it is thick enough to be pushed from the bottom of the pot with the spatula, leaving a cleared stripe for a moment. Then pour the sauce over the standing pears. Let cool and serve.

**VARIATION:**
Pears Poached in Cabernet or Merlot:
Red wine adds a blush to the pears and creates a deep red sauce. Use 1 cup of wine for 4 to 6 pears, 1 cinnamon stick instead of the lemon, and ½ cup of sugar.

fruit
fare

# 🍃fruit purées and sauces

*These recipes can become the base for fruit mousses or can be added to a trifle or a fool. They are great sauces for plain cakes or ice cream. The summer fruit adds a fresh sparkle to your desserts, while the touch of wine, liqueur, or rum helps preserve them if you want to freeze some. Frozen berries are perfectly acceptable off-season.*

## 🍃berry purée

**Makes about ½ cup**

½-pint box of raspberries, picked over and rinsed

2 tablespoons confectioners' sugar

1 tablespoon raspberry-, black-currant, or orange-flavored liqueur

**EQUIPMENT**
food processor; strainer

*T*his sauce, made with fresh raspberries, makes blushing Baked Apples (page 164), the pinkest Fruit Mousse (page 151), or a lovely red ribbon in a True Trifle (page 155). It also adds something extra to open Peach Pie (page 90).

Toss the berries into the food processor with the sugar. Pulse 10 to 15 times. Strain into a container or a serving bowl.

**QUICK TIP:**   When raspberries are at their peak and are the best bargain, double or quadruple this recipe and freeze in small batches. One preparation can make you happy many times.

**VARIATIONS:**   This same procedure works to make a Blackberry or Strawberry Purée as well. Also see recipe for Strawberries in Orange Liqueur (page 167) for another method to make Strawberry Sauce, and Mangoes in White Wine (page 169), which can be puréed into a smooth sauce as well.

i knew you were coming so i baked a **cake**

176

# blueberry sauce

*T*his is my favorite summertime topping for pound cakes or sundaes. It contrasts nicely with an open pie or tart. It can be layered with cake or ladyfingers and whipped cream for a True Trifle (page 155). Combined with Whipped Cream, it's a Fool (page 150) or Fruit Mousse (page 151). I freeze this when berries are at their peak so that I can taste summer as the leaves fall.

Add more sugar if you like this sweeter; I prefer the tartness of lemon with berries just softened by the sugar, and I like the berries mostly whole, so I stir gently. If you want to make a smoother sauce, purée in the food processor 2 or 3 pulses as it cools.

1 pint blueberries, picked over and rinsed

Juice and zest of 1 lemon (about 1 ounce and ½ teaspoon)

¼ cup sugar or 1 to 2 tablespoons honey

1 tablespoon cornstarch or 1 tablespoon tapioca

**EQUIPMENT**
strainer, 1-quart Pyrex cup and plastic wrap, or 2-quart saucepan; mixing spoon
Optional: food processor

## PROCEDURE FOR MICROWAVE:

1. Put all the ingredients into the Pyrex cup. Stir to coat the berries with the sugar and cornstarch. Cover with plastic wrap.
2. Microwave on High for 1 minute, stir, and repeat once or twice more, stirring to distribute the cornstarch and juices as they boil. The juice must boil to dissolve the cornstarch, which will thicken the sauce as it cools.

## PROCEDURE FOR SAUCEPAN:

1. Place all the ingredients in the saucepan, stir, and simmer uncovered for 5 to 10 minutes, until the juice boils and cooks off the raw taste of the cornstarch. It will thicken as it cools.

**VARIATION:** This simple sauce procedure also works well with peaches, nectarines, and plums, separately or mixed together. Dice or slice the fruit and microwave on High 1 minute at a time for 3 to 5 minutes. Pulse the mixture in a food processor to make a sauce.

The fruit skins will be broken down in the processor. If you want a purée, you can strain the skins off after processing, but I like the texture and varied colors of chunky fruit sauce.

fruit fare

# dried apricot purée

**Makes about 1¼ cups**

1 cup dried apricots

¼ cup orange juice

¼ cup orange-flavored liqueur

Juice of 1 lemon (about 1 ounce)

Confectioners' sugar (optional)

**EQUIPMENT**
2-cup Pyrex cup or 2-quart saucepan; food processor; rubber spatula

*If you keep this purée "dry" or thick, as it will be with this amount of liquid, add 2 tablespoons confectioners' sugar and it becomes apricot preserves, great for topping Almond Jam Slices (page 107), bar cookies, or plain butter cookies. Add more liquid and it makes a flavorful filling between cake layers, or in puddings, a Trifle, Fool, or Mousse.*

**PROCEDURE FOR MICROWAVE:**

1. Place the apricots and water to cover in the Pyrex cup and microwave on High for 2 minutes. Check to see if the apricots are softened. Stir and heat another minute, until they feel soft to your touch.
2. Put the softened apricots, any unabsorbed water, the orange juice, the liqueur, and the lemon juice in the food processor and pulse about 10 times, pushing the pieces down from the sides occasionally.
3. Taste and add more liquid, ¼ cup at a time, to thin the purée to an applesauce consistency, or add confectioners' sugar if you want preserves.

**PROCEDURE FOR SAUCEPAN:** Place the apricots and water in the saucepan and simmer gently until the apricots are soft, about 10 minutes. Proceed with Steps 2 and 3 above.

i knew you were coming so i baked a
**cake**

# date purée

**Makes about 1 pint**

*T*his seems very sweet, but it is great between layers of **Butter Cake** (page 30) with Caramel Sauce I (page 73), or in **Cream Cheese Cookie Rolls** (page 113). Don't decrease the amount of sugar in this recipe, because it makes syrup and binds the fruit.

1. Combine the dates, ½ cup water, sugar, lemon zest and juice, and cinnamon in the saucepan. Simmer on low heat, stirring and breaking up the dates as they soften, about 10 minutes.
2. Stir and mash the dates right in the saucepan, add the vanilla, and cool. Refrigerate or freeze for use in cookies or between cake layers.

*1 pound pitted dates*

*½ cup sugar*

*Juice and zest of 1 lemon (about 1 ounce juice and ½ teaspoon zest)*

*1½ teaspoons cinnamon*

*1 teaspoon vanilla extract*

**EQUIPMENT**
grater or zester; 2-quart saucepan; mixing spoon

# prune purée

**Makes about 1 pint**

*T*his is a great filling for **Cream Cheese Cookie Rolls** (page 113) or between layers of an **Almond Torte** (page 40).

1. Combine the prunes, ½ cup water, lemon juice and zest, and optional cardamom in the saucepan. Simmer on low heat, stirring and breaking up the prunes as they soften, about 10 to 15 minutes.
2. Stir and mash the prunes right in the saucepan. Let cool and then refrigerate or freeze.

*1 pound pitted prunes*

*Juice and zest of 2 lemons (about 2 ounces juice and 1 teaspoon zest)*

*½ teaspoon ground cardamon or 2 or 3 whole pods (remove pods after cooking) (optional)*

**EQUIPMENT**
2-quart saucepan; mixing spoon

fruit
fare

chapter 10

# bettering store-bought

## dessert cups, ladyfingers, or angel food or sponge cake

dessert cups

ladyfingers

## ANGEL FOOD OR SPONGE CAKE

strawberries romanoff

charlotte russe

## cookie crusts

pie shells

cookie cups

ice cream sandwiches

## phyllo pastry

phyllo pockets

baklava

phyllo strudel

pound cake combinations

black forest cake

## frozen puff pastry

easy as apple pie

custard fruit tart

baked fruit tart

puff pastry cookies

napoleons

sugared wontons

ricotta "mousse"

ricotta trifle

Nutella

So many wonderful products can be found these days on supermarket shelves and in their freezers. Why not use the best of these products as shortcuts to your homemade desserts?

This section has a number of ideas for adapting readily available commercial products into something special. Here's where personal tastes, time constraints, and what's in the pantry will dictate what's good and what's possible on short notice.

Leave the flour in its canister and let your homemade sauces or toppings show how you care.

# dessert cups, ladyfingers, or angel food or sponge cake

## DESSERT CUPS

These light, low-cholesterol options can support a range of delectable individual desserts. When there just isn't time to slice angel food cake or bake meringue nests, fill these with anything from an ice cream sundae or Booze Mousse (page 154) to berries with a flavored **Chantilly Cream** (page 69) or a fruit compote (see Chapter Nine).

## LADYFINGERS

I always keep a double-wrapped bag of imported Italian ladyfingers tucked way back on my pantry shelf, where they seem to keep forever. (Well, not forever; I use them and replace them periodically.) I look for them to make Tiramisù (page 157) or True Trifle (page 155), and as an accompaniment to any of the fruit, custard, or frozen recipes you will find throughout this book.

**NOTE:** In addition to the references given, check the recipes for Tiramisù on pages 157–58, True Trifle and Ricotta Trifle on page 202, Booze Mousse (page 154), and Pound Cake Combinations (page 193) for other ways to incorporate purchased cakes into homemade desserts.

# ANGEL FOOD OR SPONGE CAKE
## strawberries romanoff

**Allow for each person:**

1- or 2-inch-thick slice of angel food cake or sponge cake, three lady fingers, or one dessert cup

½ cup first-quality vanilla ice cream

1 cup Strawberries in Orange Liqueur (page 167)

🍀 Generous ½ cup of Chantilly Cream, vanilla-scented or flavored with orange, peach, or cherry liqueur

*T*his classic can be quickly assembled for crowds.

Set the cake slices on individual plates, scoop on the ice cream, and top with the strawberries and cream. Serve fast!

## charlotte russe

**Makes 6 servings**

½ an angel food or sponge cake, or 6 dessert cups

🍀 3 cups heavy cream

4 to 6 tablespoons confectioners' sugar

6 whole cherries (maraschino, canned, or frozen, defrosted, drained)

**EQUIPMENT**
3-inch biscuit cutter; electric mixer or 3-quart mixing bowl and whisk
Optional: 2-inch-wide ribbon; piping bag and star tip

*A* simple, decorative wonder created by Antonin Carême, perhaps while he cooked at Czar Alexander's court in the first third of the nineteenth century. A charlotte russe's simplicity cuts to the core of what dessert is all about: a light cake, cream whipped to stiff peaks, and a cherry on top.

My family enjoyed this treat in the early 1950s. I remember them circled with cardboard. As you licked the cream down you reached the layer of cake, which could be pushed up from the bottom of the cylinder with skilled fingers. You had to eat the cherry on top first, or very early on, or it would fall off. My sisters and I often ate ours as a mid-morning snack walking home from Saturday errands. I do not ever remember my mother, or grandmother, remonstrating that this might spoil our appetites for lunch. If anything, I think they counted on this "best part first" as an implicit contract with us to eat heartily.

i knew you were coming so i baked a **cake**

1. Slice the cake 1 inch thick, then cut out rounds using the biscuit cutter, or set out dessert cups. If you have a broad ribbon, tie it around the cake rounds or dessert cups in a bow to hide this cake layer.
2. Whip the cream with the sugar until it is quite stiff, and pile it high, swirl, curl—you might enjoy using a piping bag and tip for this one. Be sure to allow a full cup of whipped cream per portion. Indulge!
3. Top each portion with a cherry and serve immediately.

bettering
store-bought

Well, if there's no **Pâte Sucre** left in the freezer and you just can't cope, even with **Nick Malgieri's No-Roll Pie Crust** or a ready-to-bake store-bought crust, the only choice left is a preformed, no-bake cookie crust. They are readily available in graham cracker, vanilla, and chocolate cookie choices. Your guests will pay attention to these fillings, so never mind the crust.

## pie shells

- Chocolate Mousse, Version II (page 153) in chocolate cookie crust.
- Lemon Curd (page 156) topped with sliced strawberries and kiwis, in a graham cracker crust.
- Pie-sized Cheesecake (page 37) in a graham cracker crust.
- Dulce de Leche (page 75) spread thin and topped with a double recipe of Chocolate Fudge Pudding (page 149) or Mocha Pudding (page 149), garnished with chopped pecans, great in a chocolate cookie crust.
- A double recipe of Vanilla Pudding (page 143) topped with toasted coconut for coconut cream pie in a vanilla cookie crust.
- Butterscotch Sauce (pages 72–73) swirled to cover the crust, then filled with sweetened ricotta studded with rum-soaked golden raisins in a graham cracker or vanilla cookie crust.
- See other recipes under Fast Pie Fillings on pages 88–96.

## cookie cups

If you line a muffin tin with paper liners and set a vanilla wafer or biscotti on the bottom, you can make individual cheesecakes, pudding cakes, or Lemon Curd (page 156) cups to eat with a spoon. Garnish each cup with some berries on top.

# ice cream sandwiches

**Make as many as you want, using the proportions listed**

*P*ackages of soft 4-inch cookies beckoned to me near the cashiers' station one day. I bought some to try as ice cream sandwiches. Just soften your ice cream in the refrigerator for half an hour before you begin to assemble these, so the cookies don't break when pressed against hard ice cream. At an informal gathering, enlist your guests in the assembly as well as the consumption.

*2 (4-inch) cookies and ½ cup ice cream per person, in any combination of flavors that appeals to you*

*Minichips, variety of sprinkles, chopped nuts, or toasted coconut (optional)*

**EQUIPMENT**
tablespoon or ice-cream scoop; counter space or elbow room at the table

Set one cookie up and one face down. Spread ice cream at least 1 inch thick on the face-down cookie. Cover with the face-up cookie. Serve immediately. You can roll the cookie sandwich, like a wheel, through the chips or sprinkles to decorate the outer edges and serve immediately. You can wrap these in plastic wrap and refreeze the sandwiches if necessary, but most ice creams will develop some crystallization and loss of texture when refrozen.

**FLAVOR COMBINATIONS:**
- Oatmeal-raisin cookies with rum-raisin ice cream
- Dutch chocolate cookies with vanilla, chocolate, or mint chip ice cream
- Lemon cookies with strawberry ice cream, or with peach or mango sorbet
- Chocolate chip cookies with vanilla, chocolate, coffee, or cinnamon ice cream

These are safe combinations. See what exciting flavors you can find in your local ice cream store and match them with Ginger Snaps, Mint Cookies, or your other favorites for contrast.

bettering
store-bought

# phyllo pastry

Do you want to know why I like phyllo pastry? In addition to the fact that I can control the amount of butterfat I use when I work with it, here are the phyllo facts:

· You don't need flour.
· You don't need rolling pins, miles of counter space, or special equipment.
· It takes only a short baking time.
· A small knife or pair of kitchen shears is the only tool needed.
· A light touch is helpful but not required.
· You gain experience handling phyllo with the purchase and use of one box.
· There are lots of options for use.
· If it tears, just add another layer and you've fixed it.

Phyllo pastry can be found in the freezer cabinet of most grocery stores. Open a box and allow it to rest at room temperature, covered with a damp—not wet—towel for 20 to 30 minutes before attempting to handle it. Then, gently, begin to unroll the package. Do not force it, or the layers will tear, but you can allow it to rest if it is still hard. Just keep it covered with the damp towel. When it softens, unroll as much as you'll need and reroll the rest. Double wrap in plastic and refrigerate or freeze until you need it again.

i knew you
were coming
so i baked a
cake

188

# phyllo pockets

**Makes 12 servings**

*T*hese useful cups accommodate all kinds of last-minute fillings.

1. Preheat the oven to 400°F.
2. Drop 1 teaspoon of butter into each cup of the muffin tin and set the tin into the oven as it is heating.
3. Open the rolled pastry and gently place 4 layers, stacked together, flat on the cutting board. Using a paring knife or kitchen shears, cut through all the layers to make twelve 4-inch squares.
4. Remove the muffin tin from the oven. Dip the top 2 layers of each square of pastry in the melted butter in the muffin cups, then set them onto the other 2 layers. Fit all 4 layers into the muffin cup. Repeat for each of the 12 cups.
5. Bake for 10 to 15 minutes until the edges brown. Cool and remove to an airtight container lined with paper towels to absorb excess butter.
6. Fill when you're ready to serve.

**FILLINGS:**

- Sautéed Apples (page 163)
- 🍀Vanilla Pudding (page 143) topped with toasted coconut
- Fruit Mousse (page 151)
- Ice cream or frozen yogurt
- 🍀Lemon Curd (page 156)
- Fresh berries on crème fraîche or mascarpone

*4 sheets of phyllo pastry*

*¼ pound (1 stick) unsalted butter*

**EQUIPMENT**

muffin tin; cutting board and paring knife or kitchen shears; teaspoon

bettering
store-bought

**189**

# baklava

**One 8-inch square pan will make 30 to 40 1x2-inch diamond-shaped pieces; a 9x13-inch pan will make 50 to 60 1x2-inch diamond-shaped pieces.**

I cup honey

I lemon, cut up, skin and all

4 cups finely chopped walnuts

½ cup sugar

1 ½ tablespoons cinnamon

I teaspoon ground cloves

8 to 10 sheets of phyllo pastry

½ pound (2 sticks) unsalted butter

Rosewater (optional)

**EQUIPMENT**
2-quart saucepan; tablespoon; food processor or chopping knife and cutting board; clean dish towel; 1-cup Pyrex cup; 8-inch square pan or 9×13-inch pan; pastry brush; serrated knife; 4-inch spatula

*T*his is a great pastry dish, organized just like a lasagna. It does not require precision measurements, rolling pins, or even particularly fine hand skills. It gets better if it's made well ahead of time, and its procedures break easily into distinct parts that you can do whenever you have a few minutes. It is much easier to make and much more forgiving to handle than any cake I've ever made. Torn leaves of phyllo are simply layered over. (Flakes are just as tasty as perfect slices if they have been soaked in the honey syrup.) Exotic yet familiar, it's an impressive and dramatic end to a meal. Note that the smaller pan will have more layers and more height but yields fewer servings.

**DO AHEAD:**

**the syrup:**

Heat the honey with the cut lemon and 1 cup water to simmer gently about 15 minutes, until the liquid remains on the spoon with the consistency of milk. Let cool and remove the lemon pieces before using. The sauce will thicken further as it cools.

**the filling:**

Grind the walnuts with the sugar, cloves, and cinnamon in the food processor. Keep this in the refrigerator or freezer until you are ready to assemble the Baklava.

**TO ASSEMBLE:**

1. Defrost the phyllo at room temperature; open long sheets out and cut squares or rectangles to fit the pan you are using. (You can use torn or short pieces as middle layers.) Keep the phyllo covered with a slightly damp dish towel, removing sheets only when you need them.

2. Melt the butter in the Pyrex cup in the microwave for 30 seconds, stir, heat 30 seconds more, and stir again until it is all liquefied, then brush some of the butter on the bottom and sides of the pan you've selected.

i knew you were coming so i baked a **cake**

3. Place 2 layers of phyllo in the pan, and brush with butter. Add 2 layers and brush with butter. Fit extra edges of the phyllo up the sides of your pan. Layer in a third of the ground walnut mixture. Add 2 more layers of phyllo and brush with butter. (Tuck any torn pieces into the middle layer here.) Layer on another third of the nut mixture, repeat the 2-layer phyllo step, layer on the remaining nut mixture, and top with a phyllo layer and butter. Reroll the extra phyllo leaves in a plastic bag and refrigerate to use another time.

4. Bake in a preheated 350°F oven for 30 to 40 minutes until golden brown.

**TO FINISH:**

1. Warm the syrup and add the optional rosewater. Check to be sure the syrup has the consistency of whole milk (not cream, not straight honey), and add more water or lemon juice if it is too thick at this point.

2. When the baklava is golden brown and baked through, use a serrated knife to mark the 1x2-inch diamond pattern. *Do not* cut all the way through, just cut the upper layers. Pour the syrup across the entire top surface of the warm baklava so it will be absorbed and the baklava moistened throughout.

3. When the pastry has cooled and the syrup is absorbed, the serrated knife will cut all the way through the baklava to separate the sections.

**NOTE:**

I use my 8-inch square Pyrex dish so I can see the bottom browning, and my 4-inch flexible metal spatula to remove the diamonds and set them into paper petit-four cups for easier serving.

bettering
store-bought

# phyllo strudel

**Makes 6 to 8 servings**

¼ pound (1 stick) unsalted butter

2 or 3 cups your choice of filling (see below)

2 teaspoons sugar or Cinnamon-Sugar (page 22)

2 teaspoons sliced almonds (optional)

**EQUIPMENT**
cookie sheet lined with aluminum foil; 8-inch offset spatula

*I*f you don't have to make the dough, strudels don't have to be intimidating or messy.

1. Preheat the oven to 400°F.
2. Cut the butter into pats and set them on the lined cookie sheet. Put the pan in the oven to melt the butter as the oven heats. Remove when the butter is melted.
3. Place 3 layers of the pastry on a flat surface and spread 1 to 1½ cups of filling in a line along the narrow side of the pastry, leaving a 2-inch border along the edge. Bring the 2-inch border over the filling, tuck in the edges, then roll and tuck, moving up the length of the pastry. You should have a log about 8 to 10 inches long and 2 or 3 inches in diameter. Repeat with the remaining 3 sheets and filling to make a second log.
4. Use the spatula to transfer the strudel to the cookie sheet. Roll the logs over once or twice to coat the strudel with the melted butter. Sprinkle each log with 1 teaspoon sugar and the almonds, if using.
5. Bake for 25 to 30 minutes. Let cool on the cookie sheet, then use the offset spatula to transfer the strudels to a serving tray.

**FILLINGS (ENOUGH FOR 2 STRUDELS):**
- 1 can apple, cherry, or blueberry pie filling mixed with 1 can of blackberries, cherries, apricots, or Kadota figs, drained.
- 3 cups blackberries and ½ cup raspberry jam.
- ½ cup apricot jam, ½ can Kadota figs, drained, and 1 tablespoon almond paste, broken up and spread along the line of filling.
- 1 can cherry pie filling, 1 can Kadota figs, drained, and 1 tablespoon optional almond paste.

**QUICK TIP:** Lining your baking pan with aluminum foil makes for easy clean up if the filling leaks out a bit. When the strudel is transferred to a serving tray, the messy part goes right in the trash.

i knew you were coming so i baked a **cake**

# pound cake combinations

There are a number of good-quality store-bought pound cakes available, both fresh and frozen. My favorite way to serve it is toasted. The all-time best flavor and texture contrasts with this classic still seem to be the best-quality vanilla ice cream, hot fudge sauce, and cherries.

I'm a purist on this one: The cake must be served still warm with that delectable crunch of fresh crumb; it must be heavy on the ice cream, which should be allowed a few seconds to melt a few rivulets; the fudge sauce should be warm, not solidified; and, of course, the cherries go on top if you wish. (Need I suggest whipped cream before the cherry?)

I think a sauceboat, or *at least* a soup bowl, is the proper size for portion control. That leaves room for bananas sliced lengthwise if you must.

By the time everyone has eaten down to it, the pound cake is really so helpful in sopping up the "ice cream soup," you'll be glad you thought of it.

If the preceding doesn't appeal to you, you can:

· Use pound cake as the cake layer in Tiramisù (page 157) or in a True Trifle (page 155).
· Make Summer Pudding. Line the bottom and side of a loaf pan with ½-inch-thick strips of pound cake, fill with 2 to 3 cups of juicy berries. Place strips of pound cake on top and then chill at least 2 hours. Invert onto a serving plate with a rim to catch any extra juices.
· Create a spectacular Bombe. Slice pound cake ⅜ inch thick and cut into triangles. Piece the triangles together to cover the surface of a foil-lined strainer and fill with Fruit Mousse (page 151) or Chocolate Mousse (page 152). When the gelatin sets, invert onto a serving plate and peel off the foil. Then the Bombe can be covered with Jam Glaze (page 60), Chocolate Glaze (page 127), or **Whipped Cream** (page 68).
· Cover individual servings of inch-thick slices of pound cake with Rumtuffle (page 171) and garnish with a dollop of crème fraîche and Honeyed Walnuts (page 128).
· Butter and toast a thick slice of cake, douse it with ¼ cup Butterscotch Sauce (pages 72–73) and garnish with **Chantilly Cream** (page 69).
· Toast a generous slab of cake and spread it with ¼ cup **Dulce de Leche** (page 75) or Nutella, and maybe a dab of warm Microwave Fudge Sauce (page 77).

bettering
store-bought

# black forest cake

**Makes 8 to 10 servings**

*Two 9-inch round layers "Don't Do It" Chocolate Cake, two 8-inch square pans of Microwave Brownies, I pound of chocolate pound cake, or two (I-pound) boxes of prepared brownies (I prefer no nuts)*

*2 cups heavy cream*

*½ cup confectioners' sugar*

*I teaspoon vanilla extract*

*I (17-ounce) can pitted cherries, drained*

*I cup (6 ounces) semi-sweet chocolate chips*

## EQUIPMENT
electric mixer or 3-quart mixing bowl and whisk; 8-inch offset spatula; can opener; serving plate

*I*f you've had the time to whip up the **"Don't Do It"** *Chocolate Cake (page 33) or two batches of Microwave Brownies (page 51), you're already started on this one. If not, buy some chocolate pound cake or prepared brownies to start.*

1. Begin whipping the cream. As it billows, gradually add the sugar and vanilla. It's ready when it has doubled and holds stiff peaks.
2. Set one layer of cake or brownies onto your serving plate. (Remove any icing on a purchased product at this point.) Cover with whipped cream at least ½ inch thick. Spread half of the cherries and chips over the cream. Repeat for the second layer. Coat the sides with cream and set chocolate chips along the bottom edge in a 1-inch border. Decorate the top with carefully placed cherries to mark portions.

**VARIATION:**

If you really *won't* do whipped cream, try ricotta cheese beaten with ¼ cup honey, spread a bit thinner than the whipped cream.

i knew you were coming so i baked a **cake**

# frozen puff pastry

Commercial bakers and a number of fine-quality pastry firms now package terrific products like this. They're easy to use and everyone loves their crisp texture and taste. Note that puff pastry will sag in minutes when it's raining, no matter how crisp it was coming out of the oven, so if clouds threaten, try something else unless you can bake and serve your dessert almost immediately.

Set puff pastry out at room temperature about 10 minutes before attempting to work with it. Commercial package products often come with two sleeves per box, each holding pastry that is folded in thirds. The folds make it easy to use in sections, but you'll need a bit more "resting" time if you want the pastry to open out flat and remain in one piece. If the weather is warm, you'll need to move the pastry quickly to the baking stage, before it becomes soft and limp. If it does become soft, a quick trip to the refrigerator will firm it up again to handle more easily, and *it should be firm at the moment it goes into the oven*. Puff pastry should not be frozen again once thawed, but it can keep in the refrigerator several days.

bettering
store-bought

# easy as apple pie

**Makes 6 servings**

1 sheet frozen puff pastry

3 Granny Smith or Golden Delicious apples

1 teaspoon flour

2 tablespoons sugar or Cinnamon-Sugar (page 22)

1 teaspoon butter (optional)

Apricot Jam Glaze (optional) (page 60)

## EQUIPMENT

paring knife; cookie sheet lined with baking parchment or aluminum foil, or nonstick cookie sheet; serving plate
Optional: pastry brush; 1-cup Pyrex cup

*ry this French version of apple pie, a galette.*

1. Preheat the oven to 350°F. Open 1 sheet of boxed frozen puff pastry and allow it to thaw at room temperature for 10 minutes.
2. Core, peel, and slice the apples.
3. Use the pastry as a square, or cut a pastry round by trimming the whole sheet into a circular shape. Pile the trimmings on top of the edges. Put the pastry on the cookie sheet. Sprinkle the flour onto the pastry, then arrange the apples on the pastry in overlapping circles from the outer edge to the center. Top with sugar or cinnamon-sugar, and with dots of butter if you like.
4. Bake about 30 minutes. Lift the edge and check to see if the bottom of the pastry is browned and baked through.
5. Remove from the oven and allow to cool slightly. Brush with the optional glaze, heated briefly in the Pyrex cup. Serve the galette warm.

**NOTE:** See also Apple Pie (page 92).

i knew you were coming so i baked a **cake**

# custard fruit tart

**Makes 6 to 8 servings**

*P*uff *pastry can be baked unfilled and then finished with Vanilla Pudding and fresh fruits or with an array of other Fast Pie Fillings. Be sure to check underneath the pastry for a well-browned and completely baked bottom before removing it from the oven.*

1. Preheat the oven to 400°F. Open one sheet of boxed frozen puff pastry and allow to thaw at room temperature for 10 minutes.
2. Slice the pastry into thirds along the fold lines. Slice one of the thirds into 4 lengthwise strips and place 2 on each of the remaining thirds. (This creates higher edges to contain the center channel of fillings.) Place on the lined baking sheet.
3. Bake the pastry, unfilled, about 15 minutes.
4. When the pastry is baked through and browned on the bottom, remove it from the oven, let it cool, and fill the center channel of each strip with ½ cup of Vanilla Pudding and then set fruits decoratively on top. Serve as soon as possible.

**NOTE:** You can use well-drained canned apricots, peach halves, Kadota figs, or pear halves with equal success.

I sheet frozen puff pastry

I recipe Vanilla Pudding (page 143) or other Fast Pie Filling (pages 88–96)

Fruit (see Step 4 and Note)

**EQUIPMENT**
paring knife; cutting board; cookie sheet lined with baking parchment or aluminum foil, or nonstick cookie sheet

bettering
store-bought

# baked fruit tart

**Makes 6 to 8 servings**

1 sheet frozen puff pastry

Sliced apples, pears, peaches, plums, and/or berries, singly or in combination, or drained canned pears or apricots

Macaroon Topping (page 67) (optional)

Apricot Jam Glaze (page 60) (optional)

**EQUIPMENT**
paring knife; cutting board; cookie sheet lined with baking parchment or aluminum foil, or nonstick cookie sheet

1. Preheat the oven to 350°F. Open one sheet of boxed frozen puff pastry and allow to thaw at room temperature for 10 minutes.
2. Slice the pastry into thirds along the fold lines. Slice one of the thirds into 4 lengthwise strips and place 2 on each of the remaining thirds. (This creates higher edges to contain the center channel of fillings.) Place on the lined baking sheet. Arrange the fruit decoratively on the pastry or line this pastry with some Macaroon Topping (page 67) and set canned pears or apricots on top, sliced across and fanned slightly.
3. Bake for about 30 minutes. Let cool, and glaze if you wish.

# puff pastry cookies

**Makes 12 to 16 triple-stripe cookies or 3 dozen single-layer Cinnamon Swirls**

1 sheet frozen puff pastry

Sugar or Cinnamon-Sugar (page 22)

Approximately ½ cup of any of the following: chopped nuts, chocolate chips, Walnut Filling (page 54), Dried Apricot (page 178), Date (page 179), or Prune Purée (page 179), softened currants, dried cherries, or raisins (optional)

**EQUIPMENT**
cutting board and serrated knife, cookie sheets lined with baking parchment or aluminum foil, or nonstick cookie sheets

1. Preheat the oven to 400°F. Open 1 sheet of the pastry and allow to thaw at room temperature for 10 minutes.
2. Slice the pastry into 3 long strips along the folds, working while it is still cold and firm but not frozen. Generously sprinkle sugar or cinnamon-sugar onto one strip and add the optional fruit, chocolate, or nuts. Press gently into the pastry with your fingers. Top with a second strip of pastry, repeat the filling, and top with the third strip. Press firmly together.
3. Slice into ¼- to ½-inch fingers across the long strips and lay them on the lined cookie sheets with the stripes showing, leaving 2 to 3 inches between cookies. Sprinkle cinnamon-sugar or sugar on top just before baking for an extra crispy glaze. Bake 10 to 15 minutes.

**VARIATION:** For Cinnamon Swirls: Work with one-third of the pastry at a time, spread in a single layer. Totally cover the pastry with cinnamon-sugar. Slice across the width into ½-inch-thick strips, then twist and bake for a quick crunchy snack, great for an afternoon tea.

i knew you were coming so i baked a cake

# napoleons

**Makes 6 servings**

*T*hese can be assembled with frozen puff pastry or Sugared Wontons (page 200). Prepare the elements separately and combine them close to eating time to preserve the best contrast of crisp pastry and silky custard.

## DO AHEAD:
### filling:
1. Prepare the pudding and chill until you are ready for assembly.

### pastry:
2. Preheat the oven to 350°F. Open 1 sheet of pastry to thaw at room temperature for 10 minutes.
3. Slice along the folds into 3 strips. Place the strips on the lined cookie sheet.
4. Bake about 15 minutes, until golden and crispy.

## TO ASSEMBLE:
5. Whip the cream with the sugar and vanilla until it holds soft peaks. Fold the whipped cream and optional liqueur into the cooled pudding.
6. Set one strip of baked pastry on the serving plate. Layer half the lightened pudding onto the pastry, spreading an even layer ½ to ¾ inches thick to the edges, using the spatula. Repeat the pastry and pudding layers. Top with the third strip of pastry and sprinkle the extra tablespoon of confectioners' sugar on top. Cover with plastic wrap and chill 30 minutes to 1 hour.
7. Use the serrated knife and a gentle sawing motion to slice into 2-inch-thick napoleons.

**NOTE:** If you prefer, you can make Sugared Wontons (page 200) and assemble individual Napoleons. Wontons make a lighter product.

1 sheet frozen puff pastry

Double recipe Vanilla Pudding (page 143)

1 cup heavy cream

¼ cup confectioners' sugar, plus 1 tablespoon for garnish

½ teaspoon vanilla extract

1 ounce orange, raspberry, or pear liqueur (optional)

**EQUIPMENT**
cookie sheet lined with parchment or aluminum foil, or nonstick cookie sheet; electric mixer or 3-quart mixing bowl and whisk; serving plate; serrated knife; 4-inch spatula

bettering
store-bought

# sugared wontons

**The yield will depend on whether you use them whole or cut them up.**

¼ pound (1 stick) unsalted butter

1 package (16 to 20) wonton wrappers

¼ cup sugar

Cinnamon-Sugar (page 22) (optional)

**EQUIPMENT**
1-cup Pyrex cup; cookie sheet lined with aluminum foil; paring knife; paper towels; airtight container

*T*hese make a light, crispy wafer. They stay crisp in an airtight container for several days, but the instant you set them out or set them into a dish of pudding, they will soften.

1. Preheat the oven to 350°F. Cut the butter into pats directly onto the lined pan and set it in the oven to melt as the oven heats. When the butter is melted, remove the pan from the oven.
2. Use the wonton skins as they are, cut in half, into rectangles, or cut in quarters, into squares or triangles. Lay the wontons on the foil. Turn them to coat both sides with the melted butter. Generously sprinkle with sugar or Cinnamon-Sugar to cover the surface.
3. Bake 8 to 10 minutes until light golden brown and crispy. They will crisp further as they cool.
4. Remove wontons to paper towels to blot excess butter. Store in an airtight container.

**NOTE:** You can also use these as a cookie with fruit, sorbets, or custards.

# ricotta "mousse"

**Makes 4 to 6 servings**

While not whipped and lightened in the traditional fashion, this sweetened cheese (preferably made with the handmade cheese—see Note) resembles a mousse in texture.

Combine the ricotta, honey, and fruit in the mixing bowl and stir together. Mound in serving bowls and chill, garnished with additional fruit or a strawberry fan. Serve with Scots Shortbread (page 101), Butter Cookies (page 99), lady fingers, or biscotti for a fine finish.

NOTE: While supermarkets carry ricotta cheese in plastic containers at the dairy section, what I prefer for all the recipes in this book is a hand-made cheese available at specialty food shops, at some fine Italian markets, and, of course, in old Italian neighborhoods. When you taste the freshly made cheese, you might feel, as I do, that this could be dessert all by itself.

*1 pound ricotta cheese (see Note)*

*¼ cup honey or confectioners' sugar*

*2 cups fruit: a mixture of berries or a fruit purée (page 176)*

*Zest of 1 lemon (about ½ teaspoon) (optional)*

**EQUIPMENT**
2-quart mixing bowl; rubber spatula or whisk

bettering
store-bought

# ricotta trifle

**Makes 10 to 12 servings**

½ cup honey

3 pounds ricotta cheese (see Note on page 201)

1 (14-ounce) package ladyfingers, or angel cake or sponge cake sliced ¼ to ½ inch thick

½ cup rum or liqueur of your choice

¼ cup confectioners' sugar or an additional ¼ cup honey

An assortment of fruits totaling 4 to 5 cups, such as:

• 4 kiwis, peeled and sliced ¼ inch thick

• 1 (10-ounce) package frozen raspberries, blueberries, or cherries

• 2 mangoes, peeled and sliced

• 1 pint fresh strawberries, blueberries, blackberries, or pitted cherries, washed and large berries sliced

• Fruit Compotes, Loose Grapes, or fruit purées (see index) with liqueur and/or fruit juice added

**EQUIPMENT**
2- and 3-quart mixing bowls; rubber spatula; 2-quart glass serving bowl

*T*his stunning layered dessert may not be traditional, but it's certainly delicious.

1. Mix the honey into the ricotta in the 2-quart bowl.
2. In the 3-quart bowl, mix the fruit with the sugar or additional honey and the rum or liqueur.
3. Place a layer of ladyfingers or cake slices on the bottom of the glass serving bowl. Layer a third of the ricotta mixture onto this layer and top with half of the fruit mixture. Repeat these layers, ending with ricotta and just a garnish of the fruit on top.
4. Chill for at least 30 minutes before serving.

i knew you
were coming
so i baked a
cake

# Nutella

While this product has been a staple in Europe for generations, its introduction to the United States is fairly recent. Nutella is a lush chocolate-hazelnut spread that is a wonderful substitute for buttercream between layers of cake. It keeps in your pantry at room temperature. You use it directly from the jar, so it is always ready to spread if you don't have time to make an icing.

- Spread 1 cup in the middle of an **Almond Torte** (page 40) or use as a topping for Anita Farber's Banana Cake (page 34).
- Spread 1 cup between layers of **Butter Cake** (page 30) or **"Don't Do It" Chocolate Cake** (page 33).
- A tablespoon topping a cupcake will hold colorful sprinkles in place.
- Spread thinly on a baked bar cookie crust and sprinkle with chopped toasted hazelnuts.

bettering
store-bought

# Special-Needs List

**1. bettering store-bought**

In addition to Chapter 10, check these recipes:

Emergency Fruit Pie
Icings; Butterscotch Sauce III; Caramel Sauce II
Orange Couscous with Blueberries
Ricotta "Mousse"
Ricotta Trifle
Tiramisù
True Trifle
Uncooked Fruit Compotes

**2. come for brunch**

Apple Kuchen
Bar Cookies
Bread Pudding
Chocolate Chunk Bread Pudding
Coeur à la Crème
Cookie Crusts (for pies)
Crêpes
Dessert Cups, Ladyfingers, or Angel Food or Sponge Cake
Frozen Puff Pastry
Ice Cream Sandwiches
Orange Couscous with Blueberries
Phyllo Pastry
Pound Cake Combinations
Ricotta "Mousse"
Ricotta Trifle
Semifreddo
Tiramisù
True Trifle
Uncooked or Cooked Fruit Compotes

### 3. chewy and gooey

In addition to Chapter 6, see the following:

Beacon Hill Chocolate Meringues
Black Forest Cake
Blondies
Butterscotch Sauces
Caramel Sauces
Chocolate Chunk Bread Pudding
Chocolate Mousse
Cookie Crusts (for pies)
Cream Puffs
Dulce de Leche
Fruit Mousse
Granny's Oatmeal Cookies
Macaroons
Microwave Brownies
Microwave Fudge Sauce
Napoleons
Sabrina Shear's Honey Pecan Squares
Semifreddo
True Trifle

### 4. keep on hand

In addition to Chapter 7 and the Dough-Ahead section of Chapter 5, please note the Classic Cookies section in Chapter 5. In Chapter 6, all the confections hold well except Chocolate-Glazed Fruits. Also see the following recipes:

Biscuits for Personal Shortcakes
Buttercream
Chocolate Mousse, frozen as Semifreddo
Cream Puffs
Crêpes
Dulce de Leche
Fruit Purées
Lemon Curd
Nick Malgieri's No-Roll Pie Crust

i knew you
were coming
so i baked a
cake

206

Oatmeal Pecan Crisp Topping
Tiramisù

## 5. impress the empress express

Chapter 6 should do it, but if not, the Bar Cookies, Cream Cheese Cookie Rolls, and Butter Cookies with Variations in Chapter 5 may help. Here are some other suggestions:

Broiled Bananas
Caramel Pie
Dessert Cups, Ladyfingers, or Angel Food or Sponge Cake
Easy as Apple Pie
Fruit Purées
Granitas
Semifreddo
Upside-Down Berry Cake

## 6. just for drinks

Take a sweet, not savory, route with some of these recipes, perhaps serving sparkling apple cider, sparking wine, sherry, madeira wine, or a fine glass of port—especially with walnuts.

Bread Pudding
Coeur à la Crème
Frozen Puff Pastry
Honeyed Walnuts
Pound Cake Combinations
Sugar and Spice Pecans
Uncooked Fruit Compotes

## 7. kid-friendly

Just about everything in Chapter 5 and Chapter 9 will please most kids, especially Cookie Cups, Sautéed Apples, or single Fruit Compotes (generally omit the nuts and liqueurs). Some kids also go crazy for the following:

Black Forest Cake
Butterscotch, Caramel, and Microwave Fudge Sauces
Chocolate Mousse

special-
needs
list

Fools
Frozen Bananas
Fruit Crisps, no nuts
Fruit Pies
Ice Cream Sandwiches
Microwave Brownies
Pound Cake Combinations
🍀Puddings and Pudding Pies

## 8. low in cholesterol

In addition to Chapter 9, and without making a *big deal* about it, the following recipes respect this dietary constraint, but no one will feel deprived:

🍀Almond Torte (with a Jam Glaze, Juice Glaze, or a sprinkle of confectioners' sugar)
Dessert Cups, Ladyfingers, or Angel Food or Sponge Cake (fill with frozen yogurt)
Dried Fruit Truffles
Egg Whites Only Cookies
Frozen Bananas
Granitas
Honeyed Walnuts
Jam Glazes
Lemon and Orange Juice Glazes
Macaroons
Macaroon Topping
Mango Sorbet (use low-fat condensed milk)
🍀Oatmeal Pecan Crisp Topping
Phyllo Pockets (with a fruit filling)
🍀Puddings (made with skim milk)
Sugar and Spice Pecans
Sugared Wontons

## 9. minimal mess

I believe the recipes in Chapter 6 are the least fuss to clean up, but here are some others I like:

Booze Mousse
Cooked or Uncooked Fruit Compotes

Cookie Crusts (for pies)

Dessert Cups, Ladyfingers, or Angel Food or Sponge Cake (with a purchased filling like ice cream or frozen yogurt)

Dulce de Leche (served with a cookie or white cheese)

Fools

Frozen Bananas

Frozen Puff Pastry

Fruit Purées

Granitas

Jam Glazes

Nutella

Orange Couscous with Blueberries

Pound Cake Combinations

Ricotta "Mousse"

## 10. no dairy

Almost all of Chapter 9 as well as the following recipes:

Dried Fruit Truffles

Frozen Bananas

Granitas

Honeyed Walnuts

Sugar and Spice Pecans

## 11. no eggs

No eggs anywhere near the recipes in Chapter 6 or Chapter 9, or in the following recipes:

Biscuits and Personal Shortcakes

Booze Mousse

Cobblers

Dried Fruit Truffles

Frozen Bananas

Granitas

Mango Sorbet

Oatmeal Pecan Crisp Topping

Pecan Shortbreads

Phyllo Pastry

Ricotta "Mousse"

Scots Shortbread
Sugar and Spice Pecans
Sugared Wontons

## 12. no egg yolks
See Chapter 6, Chapter 7 (mostly), or Chapter 9, or try:

Almond Torte
Egg Whites Only Cookies

## 13. no heat and no sweat
Easy to assemble, even on hot, get-me-out-of-the-kitchen days:

Berry Purée
Coeur à la Crème
Dessert Cups, Ladyfingers, or Angel Food or Sponge Cake
Dried Fruit Truffles
Fools
Frozen Bananas
Ice Cream Sandwiches
Icings: Buttercream, Cream Cheese, or Sour Cream
Mango Sorbet
Nutella
Orange Couscous with Blueberries
Pound Cake Combinations
Ricotta "Mousse"
Ricotta Trifle
True Trifle
Uncooked Fruit Compotes
Whipped Cream and Flavored Whipped Creams

## 14. no oven
Use any other appliance you need:

Apple Purée
Berry Purée
Blueberry Sauce
Booze Mousse
Caramel-Pecan Candies

i knew you
were coming
so i baked a
cake

210

Chocolate-Glazed Fruit
Chocolate Mousse
Cookie Crusts (for pies)
Coeur à la Crème
✿ Crêpes
Dried Fruit Truffles
Fools
Frozen Bananas
Fruit Compotes
Fruit Mousse
✿ Fruit Purées
Granitas
Ice Cream Sandwiches
✿ Icings: Buttercream, Cream Cheese, Sour Cream
✿ Lemon Curd
Microwave Brownies
✿ Nut Brittle
Nutella
Orange Couscous with Blueberries
Peanut Butter Truffles
Pound Cake Combinations
Puddings: Chocolate Fudge, Rice, Tapioca, ✿ Vanilla
Ricotta "Mousse"
Ricotta Trifle
Sautéed Apples
Sautéed Bananas
True Trifle
✿ Whipped Cream and Flavored Whipped Cream

## 15. raid the pantry

Just when it seems that there's *nothing* in the house, check the closet, check the freezer, check these recipes:

Booze Mousse
Cookie Crusts (for pies)
Dessert Cups, Ladyfingers, or Angel Food or Sponge Cake
Dried Fruit Truffles
Granitas

Honeyed Walnuts

Nutella

Orange Couscous with (or without) Blueberries

Peanut Butter Truffles

Phyllo Pastry

Pound Cake Combinations

Puff Pastry

Puddings: Chocolate Fudge, Mocha, Rice Pudding Without the Oven,
Tapioca, Vanilla

Smooth as a Baby's . . . Carrot Cake

Sugar and Spice Pecans

## 16. come for tea
Serve it with any of the cookies in Chapter 5 or any of the following:

Apple Kuchen

Bread Pudding

Chocolate Chunk Bread Pudding

Coeur à la Crème

Cookie Crusts (for pies)

Crêpes

Date-Nut Fruit Bread

Fruit Compotes

Mom's Blueberry Muffins

Sour Cream Coffee Cake

Pound Cake Combinations

Upside-Down Berry Cake

## 17. using up the rest of whatever is left
Little bits, half portions, mystery packages, just one left—we all find "stuff"
collecting somewhere. Use it here:

Bananas—Frozen, Anita Farber's Banana Cake, Strawberry Yogurt
Muffins

Bread—Bread Pudding, Chocolate Chunk Bread Pudding

Dried Fruit—Dried Fruit Truffles, Dried Fruit Purées

Fruits—Compotes, Fools, Mousses, Trifles, Rumtuffle

Loose Grapes—Fruit Compote, Trifles, Rumtuffle

i knew you
were coming
so i baked a
cake

212

## 18. waistline-friendly

Dessert and your Size 7:

Apple Purée
Cream Puffs (light-weight fillings)
Date-Nut Fruit Bread
Dessert Cups, Ladyfingers, or Angel Food or Sponge Cake
Dried Fruit Truffles
Egg Whites Only Cookies
Fruit Compotes
Frozen Bananas
Granitas
Phyllo Pastry
Puddings (with skim milk)
Strawberry Yogurt Muffins
Sugared Wontons

## 19. yes, you can use your microwave

Parts of many recipes give directions to use the microwave to melt butter or chocolate, heat water to soften gelatin, or bring items quickly to room temperature.

These recipes can be done completely in the microwave:

Chocolate Fudge Pudding
Dulce de Leche
Fruit Compotes
Fruit Purées
Microwave Brownies
Microwave Fudge Sauce
Nut Brittle
Peanut Butter Truffles
Vanilla Pudding

# Index

index

index

# Metric Equivalencies

## Liquid and Dry Measure Equivalencies

| Customary | Metric |
| --- | --- |
| ¼ teaspoon | 1.25 milliliters |
| ½ teaspoon | 2.5 milliliters |
| 1 teaspoon | 5 milliliters |
| 1 tablespoon | 15 milliliters |
| 1 fluid ounce | 30 milliliters |
| ¼ cup | 60 milliliters |
| ⅓ cup | 80 milliliters |
| ½ cup | 120 milliliters |
| 1 cup | 240 milliliters |
| 1 pint (2 cups) | 480 milliliters |
| 1 quart (4 cups) | 960 milliliters (.96 liter) |
| 1 gallon (4 quarts) | 3.84 liters |
| 1 ounce (by weight) | 28 grams |
| ¼ pound (4 ounces) | 114 grams |
| 1 pound (16 ounces) | 454 grams |
| 2.2 pounds | 1 kilogram (1000 grams) |

## Oven-Temperature Equivalencies

| Description | °Fahrenheit | °Celsius |
| --- | --- | --- |
| Cool | 200 | 90 |
| Very slow | 250 | 120 |
| Slow | 300–325 | 150–160 |
| Moderately slow | 325–350 | 160–180 |
| Moderate | 350–375 | 180–190 |
| Moderately hot | 375–400 | 190–200 |
| Hot | 400–450 | 200–230 |
| Very hot | 450–500 | 230–260 |

i knew you were coming so i baked a cake